A PRACTICAL GUIDE
TO **SELF-HYPNOSIS**

A PRACTICAL GUIDE TO **SELF-HYPNOSIS**

by Melvin Powers

Melvin Powers
Wilshire Book Company

12015 Sherman Road, No. Hollywood, CA 91605

All Rights Reserved

Library of Congress Catalog Card Number: 61-10664
Printed in the United States of America
ISBN-0-87980-122-0

CONTENTS

FOREWORD

All of us like to think that our actions and reactions are a result of logical thought processes, but the fact is that suggestion influences our thinking a great deal more than logic. Consciously or unconsciously, our feelings about almost everything are largely molded by ready-made opinions and attitudes fostered by our mass methods of communication. We cannot buy a bar of soap or a filtered cigarette without paying tribute to the impact of suggestion. Right or wrong, most of us place more confidence in what "they" say than we do in our own powers of reason. This is the basic reason why psychiatrists are in short supply. We distrust our own mental processes and want an expert to tell us what to think and feel.

Despite this tendency to adopt our attitudes from others, man has always been dimly aware that he can influence his own destiny by directing his thoughts and actions into constructive channels. He has always, to some extent, known that his mind exerts a powerful influence on his body, and that thoughts can have harmful or helpful effects on his emotional and physical health. The ancient Egyptian sleep temples and the attempts by early physicians to drive evil spirits out of the body were both attempts to influence the body through the mind.

The unprecedented sale of *The Power of Positive Thinking* by Norman Vincent Peale and other inspirational literature proves that millions of modern people recognize the efficacy of constructive thoughts. What most of them do not recognize is that they are capable of implanting these beneficial thoughts in their own minds without reference to any outside agencies. This can be done through self-hypnosis.

In modern society we have many cults, religions and methodologies which have mental discipline as their goal. The best example of a methodology is psychosomatic medicine which deals with the interrelationship of the mind and body in the production of mental or physical illness. The rapid growth of hypnosis in the last few years is another example, and it is gratifying to see that the emphasis in this field is now shifting from hetero-hypnosis to self-hypnosis.

Self-hypnosis is a highly suggestible state wherein the individual can direct suggestions to himself. It is a powerful tool in any therapeutic process, and highly motivated subjects can parallel the success of hetero-hypnosis through their own efforts. Self-hypnosis can be used as a palliative agent and can even afford lasting results in many areas of the organism. Self-hypnosis can alleviate distressing symptoms, substitute strong responses for weak responses, help overcome bad habits, create good habits and help one's power of concentration. The total personality is eventually changed to the point where it can function adequately in an increasingly difficult environment.

In learning self-hypnosis, the subject does not relinquish control of himself as is commonly believed. Actually, more control is gained. Self-sufficiency and self-confidence are inevitable results. It is well to remember, however, that even good things may be overdone, and good judgment is necessary for favorable results. Neither hypnosis nor self-hypnosis should ever be used indiscriminately. The effectiveness of self-hypnosis depends upon many factors. Strong motivation, intelligent application of suggestions and diligence are prerequisites.

We are not suggesting that self-hypnosis can take the place of all forms of psychotherapy. We do recommend it as an adjunct to therapy when indicated. Used judiciously, it can contribute a great deal to the individual's physical and emotional well-being and happiness.

As a professional hypnotist for many years, I have seen astounding and apparently miraculous results by individuals using self-hypnosis. Many of these cases seem unbelievable to those not familiar with hypnotic phenomena. It should be remembered, though, that many individuals seek hypnosis only when all other forms of therapy have failed. This is so common that hypnosis has come to be known as a port of last call. Yet, despite the seeming hopelessness of such cases, medical literature lists thousands of remarkable recoveries.

There is nothing hit or miss about hypnosis. Used intelligently, the results are the same for all those who are properly motivated. Nor are the results singular to modern hypnotists alone. In reviewing the literature going back more than 100 years, the same gratifying results were obtained. The reader would do well to scan some out-of-print books on hypnosis at the library to understand the point further.

This book is written in terms that are comprehensible to the layman. The step-by-step instructions should afford the reader a means of acquiring self-hypnosis. The necessary material is here. The reader need only follow the instructions as they are given.

The author wishes to thank Robert S. Starrett, member of the American Medical Writers' Association, for his valuable help in the editorial preparation of this book.

It is the author's hope that you will, through the selective use of self-hypnosis, arrive at a more rewarding, well-adjusted and fuller life.

MELVIN POWERS

12015 Sherman Road
No. Hollywood, California 91605

Chapter 1

What You Should Know About Self-Hypnosis

Hypnosis has been defined as a state of heightened suggestibility in which the subject is able to uncritically accept ideas for self-improvement and act on them appropriately. When a hypnotist hypnotizes his subject, it is known as hetero-hypnosis. When an individual puts himself into a state of hypnosis, it is known as self-hypnosis. In both cases, the subject has achieved a heightened state of suggestibility. Even in hetero-hypnosis, the subject really controls the response to suggestions. Actually, all hypnosis is really a matter of self-hypnosis. The subject enters into the hypnotic state when he is completely ready to do so. This may require from one to many attempts before it is achieved. Even if the subject insists that he wants to be hypnotized immediately, he may be resisting hypnosis unconsciously.

In self-hypnosis the same thing usually takes place. The subject is anxious to achieve self-hypnosis, but somehow the state eludes him. What's wrong? It may be that he is

unconsciously resisting it, hasn't conditioned himself sufficiently, or has achieved the hypnotic state and doesn't
know he is in the state. This last statement may be sur-
prising, but we will examine it in detail a little later on.

Most experts agree that about 90 percent of the popula-
tion can be hypnotized. My own feeling is that probably
99 percent can be hypnotized. Who among us is not influenced by suggestion? Aren't we all, as we have seen,
influenced by the suggestions of advertising? Don't we all
have a tendency to believe what we read in the paper, hear
on the radio or see on television? Aren't we all convinced
that a name-brand article is better than one that is not so
well-known?

Suggestion plays a tremendously important role in our
daily lives. It begins from naming the baby with an appropriate name to securing a suitable place for interment. I
would like to call the reader's attention to a fascinating
book dealing with the unconscious reasons why we do
many of the things that we do. You will be intrigued with
every page of the book. It is called *The Hidden Persuaders*
by Vance Packard.

My contention is that we are all suggestible and, therefore, being hypnotized or hypnotizing ourselves is just a
matter of increasing the suggestibility that we already possess. Doesn't the hypnotist begin by suggesting relaxation?
Doesn't he usually begin by requesting the subject to fix
his attention on a particular object? Next, he suggests to
the subject that his eyes are becoming heavy and tired.
As soon as the subject closes his eyes, he suggests that he
will be in a deep hypnotic state. I am sure that you are
familiar with this procedure. With each step, the hypnotist is guiding the subject along directed lines to get him
to accept further suggestions without question or doubt.

When the subject achieves the ultimate state in this procedure, he has been hypnotized. He then accepts suggestions without equivocation.

Let us continue with this same thought. Suppose I say to you, "I'm going to stick you with this pin. It won't hurt." Would you let me stick you with the pin? Obviously not. Let us suppose that you have been hypnotized and I repeat the same suggestion. What happens then? You readily accept the suggestion as being factual. Should I proceed to stick you with the pin, you do not even flinch. In fact, you do not even feel the pain. Does this sound incredible? Isn't this exactly the same procedure that the dentist uses with his patient when he has hypnotized him for the purpose of painless dentistry?

Achieving hypnosis, therefore, is a matter of directing this suggestibility that we all possess into the channels that will finally produce the hypnotic state. It can be much more complicated than this explanation in many cases, but let us use this as a working premise.

Everyone can be hypnotized. The time required for achieving hypnosis will vary from subject to subject. We will discuss some of the reasons for this in a subsequent chapter, but for our discussion at this time we need to understand this point. I have encountered numerous individuals who were extremely disappointed because they did not respond to hypnosis immediately or after several attempts. They wanted to know "what was wrong." An explanation that nothing was wrong somehow did not satisfy these individuals. "After all," they argued, "didn't I go to a hypnotist especially to be hypnotized?" Some insinuated that perhaps the hypnotist wasn't too good.

Let me explain that most subjects need to be conditioned for hypnosis, and this conditioning is helped when the subject practices certain conditioning exercises that I shall discuss in detail in chapter six, titled "How To Attain Self-Hypnosis." In my teaching, I have found that about one out of ten subjects responds to the first attempt at hypnosis. One cannot make a definite statement as to the length of time necessary to learn self-hypnosis, but it is my experience that this usually takes about one month. I have had subjects learn self-hypnosis in about 30 minutes, but I must also relate that I have worked with subjects for one year before they achieved it.

For the most part, the laws of learning apply to self-hypnosis as with anything else that one would want to learn. It can be a relatively simple procedure, or it can be very perplexing. The answer lies not so much with the hypnotist as with the subject.

One question that arises is: "If I'm under hypnosis, how can I give myself suggestions?" During the hypnotic state, it must be remembered, the subject is always aware of what is going on. He hears what is said, follows directions and terminates the state when told to do so. In the self-hypnotic state, the subject is in full control. Therefore, he can think, reason, act, criticize, suggest or do whatever he desires. He can audibly give himself suggestions, or he can mentally give himself suggestions. In either case, he does not rouse from the hypnotic state until he gives himself specific suggestions to do so. Many feel if they audibly give themselves suggestions, they will "awaken." In hypnoanalysis, the subject answers questions during the hypnotic state. Having the subject talk does not terminate the state. You can keep the talkative subject under hypnosis as long as you want. Furthermore, the subject can be sitting erect with his eyes open and still be under hypnosis. Carrying this further, the subject may not even be aware that he is under hypnosis. He can be given a cue not to remember when the therapist makes a certain motion or says a certain word that he will go back into the hypnotic state but still keep his eyes open. Only an experienced hypnotist could detect the change.

Another frequent question is: "How do I arouse myself from the self-hypnotic state?" You merely say to yourself that upon counting to five you will open your eyes and wake up feeling fine. Many times the subject falls asleep while giving himself posthypnotic suggestions. This is not undesirable since the suggestions will spill over into the subconscious mind as he goes from consciousness to unconsciousness.

A popular opinion about hypnosis is that the subject surrenders his will to the hypnotist in the process of being hypnotized. Furthermore, many believe that once the subject is hypnotized, the hypnotist has complete control of the subject and the subject is powerless to resist suggestion. Both beliefs are erroneous. I believe the first misconception comes from seeing techniques where the hypnotist requests the subject to look into his eyes. The hypnotist suggests to the subject that as he continues to look into his eyes he will fall into a deep hypnotic state. This, then, becomes a matter of who can outstare whom. The subject usually begins to blink his eyes and the hypnotist follows this up with rapid suggestions that the subject's eyes are becoming watery and heavy and that the subject will fall into a deep hypnotic sleep just as soon as he (the subject) closes his eyes. This procedure gives the impression to the observer that the subject is "willed" to go under hypnosis. It appears that once the hypnotist concentrates or wills sufficiently, the subject succumbs. Actually, the hypnotist in this technique is not looking into the eyes of the subject.

He fixes his attention on the bridge of the nose of the subject.

The concept that the subject is a helpless automaton stems from the weird movies where the "mad scientist" has hypnotized subjects into behaving like zombies. Naturally, there is usually a beautiful girl in the movie and she, too, has been hypnotized. Even though the audience is sophisticated enough to realize that this science-fiction drama is purely entertainment, the theme is repeated sufficiently in novels, comics, and television to make an indelible impression on the subconscious mind. It's the technique of telling the "big lie" so many times that it becomes believable. We are all influenced by this procedure. There is an excellent book explaining this very premise. It is called *Battle For The Mind* by William Sargent. It describes in detail the technique by which evangelists, psychiatrists, politicians and advertising men can change your beliefs and behavior.

Following the reasoning that the subconscious mind can be affected, you can see that a problem could present itself even though the subject consciously wishes to be hypnotized. Unconsciously, there may be a poor interrelationship with the hypnotist which can create an unfavorable climate for hypnosis. When this is the case, the subject doesn't respond until such time that he relates well to the hypnotist. Even the most calculated procedures will fail until a positive transference relationship is established. I am sure that you sometimes have said, "For some reason I don't like that person." If pressed for an answer, you'll usually reply, "I can't explain it, but I just have a feeling about him." Actually, your subconscious reactions are influencing your thinking and you "feel" a certain way. The same thing takes place in business transactions. You either like or dislike the proposition presented to you. You may say, "I have a certain feeling about this deal." You may not be conscious of the reasons, but your subconscious has reacted automatically because of previous experience along similar lines.

In giving you some insight into the hypnotic procedure, I am trying to point out certain problems in regard to acquiring self-hypnosis. For the most part, it is not a simple procedure that is accomplished immediately. You can't just will it. It requires working toward a specific goal and following definite procedures which eventually lead to success.

The hypnotist is usually endowed by the subject with an omniscience and infallibility which logically is unjustified. The subject is naturally extremely disappointed if he doesn't respond immediately. If he loses confidence in the hypnotist, he may never achieve hypnosis with this particular hypnotist. I have hypnotized subjects who have been to several other hypnotists without success, and I have had some of my unsuccessful subjects hypnotized by other hypnotists. How and why does it happen? I believe that some of the reasons are so intangible that it would be impossible to explain all of them with any degree of exactitude.

I once saw an individual about 12 times who wanted to learn self-hypnosis and had been unsuccessful in every approach. I asked him if he would volunteer as a subject for a class in techniques of hypnosis that I was teaching for nurses. He readily volunteered and showed up at the designated time. Much to my amazement as well as his own, he responded within a relatively short time as one of the nurses hypnotized him before the group. She had used a standard eye closure technique, requesting him to look at a spinning hypnodisc that I had previously used with him every time he was in the office. Her manner was extremely affable, she had used the identical technique I had used unsuccessfully, and the subject responded excellently to cap the climax. He was the first subject the nurse had ever hypnotized, since this was only her third lesson.

How would you account for it? Here was one of my students with two weeks' experience hypnotizing a subject where I had failed while using every procedure that I felt would work. Was it because she was a better hypnotist? Perhaps! However, I'd like to recall at this time our discussion about subconscious responses. I'm inclined to feel that being hypnotized by a middle-aged female nurse created certain favorable unconscious responses which accounted for his going under hypnosis at that time. It created the initial break-through which was needed. I was able to hypnotize him easily at his next appointment, and he acquired self-hypnosis readily from that time on.

I have tried the same approach with other subjects who did not respond favorably and have failed to attain the success that I did in the above case. Why the impasse? It is one of the difficulties that we encounter in hypnosis, and as yet it has not been resolved.

We know that the easiest way to achieve self-hypnosis is to be hypnotized and given a posthypnotic suggestion that you will respond to hypnosis by a key word, phrase or gesture. I have tried to point out some problems that can arise. Needless to say, these problems do not always arise, and the attainment of self-hypnosis can be a relatively simple procedure. There is usually some way of reaching a subject who does not respond in a reasonable length of time.

Now we come to the point where the subject wishes to

hypnotize himself. What happens in this situation? It would appear that the subject would go under hypnosis immediately. After all, isn't he controlling the hypnotic session? Of course, this does happen time and time again, and the results seem miraculous. I receive mail constantly from readers of several of my other books on hypnosis telling me how they were able to achieve certain goals that they never dreamed possible. They write that they have achieved self-confidence and complete self-mastery and have been able to overcome problems that have plagued them for many years. These problems not only include strictly psychological troubles but many psychosomatic symptoms as well. Many have remarked at the ease in which they were able to achieve self-hypnosis and the results they wanted. For them it was as simple as following a do-it-yourself book.

Others write about the difficulty they encounter and ask what to do about it. It is my hope that this book will shed some light for those who have experienced difficulty in learning self-hypnosis. We shall discuss many phases of hypnosis with the emphasis on self-hypnosis. We'll discuss its many ramifications and try not to leave out anything helpful in our discussion.

If you follow the instructions and exercises that I give you assiduously, you should be able to achieve a depth of self-hypnosis suitable for solving many of your personal problems.

Chapter 2

What About the Dangers of Hypnosis?

One of the objections that you hear to hypnosis is that it can be dangerous in the hands of those not trained in the psychodynamics of human behavior. Inasmuch as psychiatrists and clinical psychologists are the only ones who are thoroughly trained in the analysis of human behavior, this objection, if valid, could limit hypnosis to a comparative handful of therapists. Fortunately, it is not valid. This was proved several years ago when the "Bridey Murphy" craze gripped the country. Despite the fact that thousands of amateur hypnotists were practicing hypnosis, little or no harm resulted. I have personally instructed several thousand medical and non-medical individuals and have yet to hear of a single case where a crisis was precipitated or anything of a dangerous or detrimental nature occurred as a result of hypnosis. I have also taught several thousand persons self-hypnosis and can report the same findings.

Many patients who seek treatment from competent

psychiatrists, psychoanalysts and psychologists do not always obtain satisfactory results. This doesn't mean that everyone should stop seeking help from these specialists. Even a specialist doesn't have a perfect record of successful therapy.

What then is the objection to hypnosis? The theory that if you get rid of one symptom another symptom will take its place really holds no truth and is usually advanced by those who have had little or no experience in the hypnosis field. However, a difference of opinion does exist even with those practicing hypnosis in this area. Some hypnotists "trade down" symptoms by replacing a serious symptom with a minor one, while others just remove the symptom. The latter is what a doctor does when he recommends aspirin for arthritis. He knows the aspirin will not cure the arthritis, but he wants to alleviate the symptom. To say that another symptom will replace the pain is unscientific — and untrue. The same is true of hypnosis.

Lewis R. Wolberg, M.D., clinical professor of psychiatry, New York Medical College, recently canvassed 30 experts in the field of hypnosis and found a few who felt symptom removal was "irrational, temporary — or outright dangerous." The large majority, however, "employed symptom removal where indicated, and minimized or ridiculed any possible bad effects."

A further objection to hypnosis is that the results are temporary as well as symptomatic. It is well to remember that most medical therapy is specifically directed to symptom removal. How permanent is most medical treatment? Once you couple heterohypnosis with self-hypnosis, you afford the patient the opportunity of utilizing suggestions for his own benefit any time they are needed. This, of course, can make symptom relief permanent. As an example, I would see no harm in teaching a patient self-hypnosis for symptomatic relief from a problem of insomnia. It would certainly be better than physically depressing the higher brain centers with sleeping pills to produce unconsciousness every night. I needn't tell you that millions of dollars are spent every year on sleeping pills and patients become dependent upon them, needing more and more pills in order to produce sleep. Many accidental suicides stem from an overdose of sleeping pills. Yet, despite the inherent dangers of sleeping pills which are glaringly apparent, they are prescribed by the millions, to say nothing of those that reach the market through illegal channels. Furthermore, how much effort is really made to get the patient off the sleeping pills? There are also more voluntary suicides by sleeping pills than by any other method. Perhaps if these drugs weren't so readily available, many of these unfortunate individuals would be with us today.

What about the often-quoted statement that "you might do some damage"? Let's explore this area. I assume that the reader is somewhat familiar with the work of Emile Coué or at least has heard of his famous autosuggestion formula of "Day by day, in every way, I'm getting better and better." During our time, thousands upon thousands of seemingly helpless and hopeless cases have been cured by repeating this affirmation over and over again, day after day, as the individual falls asleep.

I think we should make it clear that whether we call it autosuggestion, positive thinking, meditation, yoga, affirmations or self-hypnosis, we are, in reality, talking about the same thing. All require certain basic prerequisites before they will work effectively for the individual. We'll

23

discuss these prerequisites in the next chapter.

What should be remembered is that the suggestions are being filtered into the subconscious mind which does not question, doubt, analyze or dispute the efficacy of these beneficial thoughts. You can be sure that the constant repetition will have its effect. Hasn't the mind, in the past, accepted the individual's diagnosis when he said, "I'm sick," "I have an inferiority complex," "I can't stop smoking," "I can't lose weight," "I can't concentrate," "I can remember a person's face, but I can't remember names," "I have a difficult time falling asleep," "I just can't seem to relax." Isn't such an individual, in effect, using self-hypnosis? And hasn't the person convinced himself of the validity of his present state? This is truly dangerous. It is negative hypnosis.

The question that I raise is: "Why shouldn't the subconscious mind be even more convinced and respond strongly to suggestions which are in conformity with the natural desire to be of sound body and mind?" I have never been able to find a logical answer.

I think this is what happens many times. A person seeks help with a problem which, in reality, has nothing to do with hypnosis. His cure is not contingent on being hypnotized or on suggestions he or the hypnotist feel are indicated. You will read in nearly every book and article dealing with hypnosis that "hypnotism is not a cure-all." No one has suggested or implied that it should be used exclusively for all emotional problems. You may read a newspaper article warning about the "dangers" of hypnosis. It may tell of a person who rid himself of one symptom and developed another in its place. You usually get a grossly distorted picture of what happened, with many aspects of the case not included. It's a matter of taking what you want to prove out of context. Propagandists use this technique all the time to get across their message. It's the old story of telling a half truth.

Honest criticism and a sincere difference of opinion are always welcome. But criticism must be well-founded from a scientific point of view and not stem from an emotional reaction. You have probably heard the remark, "I won't let anyone hypnotize me." What are they really saying, and what does hypnosis represent to such an individual? To them, hypnosis represents some sort of "magic spell" which invokes a state of complete helplessness and dependency upon the hypnotist. We previously discussed how this erroneous conception can take place because of the manner in which hypnosis is usually interwoven with bizarre fictional stories.

For many, the hypnotic state represents a period in which the conscious guard is dropped. They feel they may compulsively reveal the darker side of their nature, confess their hostility or relate information they would never voluntarily divulge to anyone. This is the real danger they see in hypnosis. To protect themselves from it, they attack it. It is much like the fanatic vice crusader who militantly attacks sin in order to alleviate his own feelings of guilt stemming from the fact that vice actually attracts him.

Fear of hypnosis takes different forms, but basically it is the fear of revealing one's true feelings. An employee, for instance, at a gathering which included the employer he dislikes, would never volunteer as a subject for hypnosis if the occasion arose. He would be afraid he would do or say something which might endanger his position. Hypnosis for him would be "dangerous" because he would be afraid to take the chance. The truth is, however, that this individual would be taking no chance. The hypnotic state is not a confessional period. The subject is aware at all times of what he is saying. If the subject does not wish to pursue a line of questioning, he tells the hypnotist. If the hypnotist persisted further along this line, the subject would shake off the hypnotic state.

Another misconception about hypnosis is the widely held belief that the subject is unconscious. This represents a threat to the security of the individual. Actually, the hypnotic state is a period of extreme awareness in which the subject is hyperacute. Furthermore, the subject is not asleep, nor is he in a trance state in the correct meaning of that term. He is in an altered state of awareness with his faculties and reasoning ability intact. Inducing hypnosis merely creates a mood or state in which the powers of suggestibility are heightened.

When the general public and the medical profession become familiar with the true nature of hypnosis, we shall have a greater acceptance and utilization of this power. It is a slow process but one which will finally evolve. In the final analysis, I believe the only danger that exists is in the mind of the individual who fears hypnosis because of whatever subjective qualms he has about his own emotional involvement in the hypnotic process.

Of course, all persons using hypnosis for the alleviation of pain should consult their family physician. Pain is nature's way of indicating that something is wrong with the organism. It would be foolish to suggest that a pain in the stomach will disappear when this may be a sign of a needed appendix operation. The same may be said of constant migraine headaches. It must be determined that the headache is not a symptom of a brain tumor or some other pathological condition. It may be of interest to know that hypnosis is presently being used to relieve pain in terminal cancer patients. There is an excellent article on this subject, and I recommend it to doctors reading this book. It is called "The Use of Hypnosis in the Case of the Cancer Patient" which appeared in the January 1954 issue of *Cancer*.*

There are at present several thousand dentists throughout the country using hypnosis. They have formed their own society and publish a quarterly journal, *The Journal of the American Society of Psychosomatic Dentistry*. One of the best books in this field is called *Dental Hypnosis Handbook* by Jacob Stolzenberg, D.D.S.

An excellent article is "Danger! Hypnotherapist at Work" by M. Abramson.† The author reviews briefly the pros and cons regarding the medical use of hypnosis. He concludes: "It is the author's opinion, based on an extensive personal experience of over 15 years, that the use of hypnotherapy by a physician or dentist who has been properly trained and who uses this technique strictly within his field of competence carries with it no more (and probably less) 'danger' than the use of many other techniques of treatment used in medicine today."

*At the same time, I would highly recommend the booklet, *Helping the Dying Patient and His Family*, published by the National Association of Social Workers, 2 Park Avenue, New York 16, New York. Price: 75 cents.

†Bull. Hennepin Co. Med. Soc., 1960,31:101-106

Chapter 3

Is Hypnosis the Answer?

Dr. George Estabrooks, professor of psychology at Colgate University and author of the book, *Hypnotism,* made the following two statements in a paper called "The Future of Hypnosis" given as part of a program on "The Nature of Hypnosis" at the annual meeting of the American Psychological Association in 1959:

"It would be well to sound a word of caution against certain attitudes which have become prevalent and which can be well illustrated in the field of medicine. In this respect, direct suggestion is under the ban. For example, a dictum, 'Never remove the symptom unless the cause is understood,' is much emphasized. Its validity is greatly open to question, since much of medical practice is direct symptom removal, as only a little thought makes apparent.

"Another dictum generally followed is that the unconscious background of symptom-complexes must necessarily be made conscious to effect a cure. Reasonable and thoughtful consideration of the extensive role of the unconscious in daily living and functioning renders this dictum much less creditable."

I should like to discuss both of these statements in some detail as they invariably arise in the mind of the individual seeking help through hypnosis.

The first thought that comes to mind is that all the religious healings cited in the Bible involve direct symptom removal. The cures that are effected by religious devotees traveling to sacred shrines are also in the realm of direct symptom removal. I have yet to hear a criticism of this type of treatment directed at religious leaders or condemnation of the religious shrines. These cures are accepted as evidence of the power of faith or attributed to the supernatural. In these cases, nothing is ever done to make the person cured understand the nature of the unconscious mechanisms which contributed to his problem.

Religious healing cannot be dismissed by merely saying, "It isn't scientific." A methodology is only scientific when it works. It is of no value if it doesn't help the individual seeking help. We must face the fact that not all people can be helped by the same psychological treatment. We can readily see this in the following extreme example: An aborigine suffering from a psychological problem certainly wouldn't be a candidate for psychoanalysis as we know it. He could, no doubt, be helped much more readily by a witch doctor. It also stands to reason that the sophisticated Westerner would not be influenced by the incantations of a tribal medicine man.

Going further, we find there are many schools of psychotherapy and many approaches to solving man's emotional problems. The cure rate for all of them, however, is approximately the same. I think we must accept the fact that there is no *one* sound, logical, scientific approach.

I believe that so long as the end result is achieved, the methodology was scientific for that individual's needs. The goal of all therapies is to help the patient free himself from whatever emotional problems beset him.

This approach, to some readers, may seem an oversimplification of a very complex problem, but I think it's time that we had a simple, workable formula devoid of technical jargon. Too often, complex technical terms and theories have been glibly used to explain away failures. I believe we need more and more emphasis on measures to make the patient feel better rather than spending most of the time trying to find out why he doesn't feel well. This, of course, is symptom removal again.

I should like to point out an interesting fact pertaining to Biblical healers. So long as the fame of the healer preceded his arrival in any country, he was able to heal the sick. However, where his fame as a healer was either unknown or discredited, he found no faith and subsequently no cure. The earliest reference to hypnosis is in the Bible, Genesis ii, 21. "And the Lord God caused a deep sleep to fall upon Adam, and he slept..."

Dr. William Malamud, 86th president of the American Psychiatric Association, in an address delivered at the annual meeting in 1960, stated the following in a paper called "Psychiatric Research: Setting and Motivation":

"During the last few years we have witnessed a growing trend of overemphasizing the value of 'exact' methodology and uniformity of standards. This trend, which could be characterized as a 'cult of objectivity,' has already had an important influence on psychiatric research. It is true that in its emphasis on critical judgment and valid criteria, it has helped to curb unrestrained flights of imagination and sloppy methodology. But the overglori-

31

fication of objectivity and the insistence on rigidly single standards of acceptable methods have resulted in a concentration on certain phases of the science of human behavior at the expense of other very important ones."

I believe that most individuals have a fairly good understanding of how they came to have the problem that they have. I have yet to encounter the person who protests he has no idea why he doesn't function as he would like to in a certain area. From a practical standpoint, not many have the time nor money required to delve into the unconscious background of the problem. The high cost of treatment is a very real objection and cannot be discounted lightly. People suffering from emotional problems usually suffer financial reverses as well. Who is to help these people? There are very few places in the country where they can receive competent psychiatric help at a reasonable fee. Is there this type of help in your own community? It is only when the individual is destitute that the state provides whatever help it can. However, at this point it's a long hard struggle back to good emotional health.

The National Association for Mental Health and its affiliates issue about 10 million copies of 200 different pamphlets on various aspects of mental health. To assess the value of these pamphlets, 47 mental hygiene experts held a conference at Cornell University. A report on this outstanding conference has been published. It is called "Mental Health Education: A Critique." A feature by Ernest Havemann in the August 8, 1960 issue of *Life* contains a very worthwhile article on this conference called "Who's Normal? Nobody, But We All Keep On Trying. In Dissent From 'Mental Health' Approach, Experts Decry Futile Search For An Unreal Goal." The following paragraph is taken from the *Life* article:

"What about psychiatry and psychoanalysis? This is a different matter. Many unhappy and problem-ridden people, though by no means all who have tried it, have profited from psychotherapy. Indeed, all the mental health pamphlets, as a postscript to the self-help methods they advocate, wind up by advising the reader to seek professional care if his problems are serious enough. But the skeptics at Cornell cited statistics which to them show that psychiatric treatment is as remote for the average person as a trip to the moon. Aside from the expense, which most people would find prohibitive, there simply are not enough therapists to go around. The U. S. has around 11,000 psychiatrists and 10,000 clinical psychologists — in all, about one for every 8,500 citizens. If everybody with emotional problems decided to see a psychiatrist, the lines at the doctors' offices would stretch for miles."

I assume that most readers of this book know that state hospitals are understaffed and unable to provide proper care for the mentally ill. Mike Gorman, executive director of the National Mental Health Committee, has written a crusading report on this very theme called *Every Other Bed*. In this book he tells us that every other hospital bed in the United States is occupied by a mental case. Mental illness costs the country two and a half billion dollars a year besides the more important untold human suffering that can never be equated in dollars. The book is a shocking story of how we have let this happen; are still letting it happen; and of how little, for the most part, we, the general public as well as the medical and psychological professions, are doing to correct this deplorable situation.

It is time that we re-examined the dictums that say a symptom can never be removed unless the cause is understood and the unconscious background of symptom-complexes must be made conscious and understood before a cure is effected.

There are many positive thinking groups functioning in the religious field. Many of these religious groups are in existence primarily because of the dynamic philosophy or psychology they offer for every day living. Couple this with a strong faith in God, and you have a combination which approaches infallibility. Recently we have had a series of best-selling books which expound this very theme. Does it work? Of course it does when used properly.

You can be sure that there has been criticism of this religious psychology. The criticism is that the basic causes of the problem are never dealt with and the unconscious conflict is not resolved. It's the same argument over and over again. What about the people helped? They seem to have made tremendous strides and are leading lives as well adjusted as anyone else. Once imbued with this spirit or feeling of well-being, it permeates every phase of their relationships in a constructive manner. The only reason that there isn't more criticism is that this type of psychotherapy is incorporated into the religious tenets of these groups, and criticizing another man's religion makes the detractor's entire philosophy unacceptable. I am strongly in favor of these groups because I would prefer having a religion that keeps pointing out the positive side of life and that "life can be beautiful" if you put your faith in God and practice positive thinking. It is certainly better than the cynical philosophy of its detractors or the grim religions which stress punishment. Think of the guilt feelings involved in the latter. No one can live up to such a formidable creed.

Of course, if you suggest to positive thinking, religious individuals that they are using a form of self-hypnosis, they will emphatically deny and debate the issue. Since we are primarily interested in mental hygiene and not in winning a debate, it is well to leave the matter as it stands. The point to keep in mind is that so long as a person feels that this methodology is the answer to his needs and so long as no one is being hurt by his belief, I feel he should cling to his conviction. He should not allow it to be destroyed by those who are thinking in different semantic terms.

I would like to bring up another common example pertaining to the two basic concepts that we have been discussing. It is the example of the many individuals who have taken public speaking courses to overcome stage fright. In most cases, the person involved hasn't had too much opportunity to be a public speaker. Because of this, he suddenly feels he may not say the right thing or forget what he wants to say. This anxiety can create the very situation or block that he fears. What is the solution? Certainly not psychoanalysis to find out why he functions the way he does. You could use this approach, but I don't think it's the most constructive one. It is like asking, "What am I doing that's wrong?" instead of "What can I do that's right?" The most constructive approach is to take a course of instruction to get the actual practice and experience in the techniques of public speaking.

Before proceeding further, I believe it is necessary to point out that I am not just being critical of the convictions of other sincere and dedicated individuals engaged in the field of mental hygiene. It is always good to reevaluate our present thinking on any subject, no matter how sincere or convinced we may be that what we are doing is correct. At times, we can become so immersed in our convictions that we cannot take criticism and respond emotionally to ideas or interpretations that do not coincide with logical thinking.

What, then, is the answer to mental health problems? There is no single answer. It is a very complex situation. There are many promising drugs and treatments which, if adequately developed and widely used, could do a great deal toward promoting good mental health. Fundamentally, the problem will always be that of trying to understand human behavior and helping those in distress with an efficacious formula.

What is that formula? I believe hypnosis can contribute in part to the answer. Needless to say, hypnosis is contraindicated in many emotional problems because of the very nature of the problem itself. Some emotional difficulties must first be worked out on a conscious level. After this, hypnosis can be instrumental in achieving the final goal.

Dr. Frank S. Caprio, a prominent psychiatrist, in his book, *Helping Yourself with Psychiatry*, states the following: "A whole new world of self-confidence and positive living is open to every person, young and old, through hypnosis, self-hypnosis and self-suggestion or auto-hypnosis."

Chapter 4

How Does Self-Hypnosis Work?

There's an old Chinese proverb that states: "One picture is worth a thousand words." In conveying suggestions to the subconscious, we have found that picture images are more effective than the words that are implanted. For example, it isn't sufficient to say, "I will be confident." The words must be augmented by a picture of yourself as the confident person you want to be. If you say, "I can't visualize myself as a confident person because I have never been that way," you can "borrow" those personality traits that you want for yourself. Imagine yourself endowed with the characteristics of some confident person that you know. The qualities that you seek may even be borrowed from a famous person. If this isn't possible, make up a personality which is a composite of all the things you want to be. See yourself walking, talking and carrying on activities. Keep fortifying this image with the mental suggestions that are needed. It won't be long before these mental impressions give rise to the confident feelings that you seek. As you keep implanting these images, they will become a natural part of your conscious personality.

Dr. S. J. Van Pelt, president of the British Society of Medical Hypnotists and editor of the *British Journal of Medical Hypnotism,* writes about this technique in his book, *Secrets of Hypnotism.* He calls it " '3-D' Technique in Medical Hypnotherapy." As you read the following paragraph, it would be well to remember that it contains the essence of making the self-hypnosis technique work once you have achieved the hypnotic state, per se. Incidentally, the same procedure can be used in attaining the hypnotic state itself. You see yourself entering the state of hypnosis in your initial attempts. This, in turn, sets up a conditioned response and a favorable emotional reaction which is necessary.

"The writer has found (visualization) of the greatest value in the re-education of the patient, which is an essential part of hypnotherapy. In this method, after the cause of the trouble has been discovered and as a part of his re-education, the patient is instructed while under only light hypnosis to 'form a picture' in his mind. He is asked to imagine a movie screen and to see himself 'just like an actor' on this screen playing a part. He is told that the picture looks 'very real'—'3-D' in fact — and that he can see himself acting and looking the way he really wants to look and act. Various scenes are suggested such as . . . the patient will have to face in real life. In each he is instructed to see himself —'as in real life'— always succeeding. For instance, the stammerer might be asked to picture himself speaking easily to people, and feeling perfectly at ease. The patient is also instructed how to form these 'success pictures' for himself, and it is stressed that he will only be able to see himself as he wants to be — successful. Since the pictures give rise to the appropriate feelings, it is not long before the patient begins to show the benefit of his private '3-D' film shows."

After explaining this technique to students, many have inquired, "Is that all there is to it? It seems so simple." Of course, there is more to it in that the individual must follow through with the instruction. This is one of the difficult aspects of this type of program. Let me enumerate some of the problems I have encountered in teaching self-hypnosis.

As mentioned, one of the difficulties is that the technique seems too simple. Students become skeptical. They feel it should be more complicated and involved in order to get results. I suppose people better appreciate something that comes only after a hard struggle. This procedure is devoid of this. Of course, I am not saying that once a person begins to use this technique his problems will automatically vanish and his life will be cheery forever after. We have been conditioned to think that success in anything can only come after a long, hard struggle. This is the basic theme of the American way of life. We have been accustomed to believe that conflict and struggle are part of life and large doses of it are necessary before we achieve success in any field. I can only reiterate that the information contained in this book is all you need to get results. It is necessary that you follow through and not give up after you have tried the program for a short while and have obtained no appreciable results. This brings us to another point.

Many persons expect immediate results when they begin to use self-hypnosis. If they don't get the results they anticipated immediately, they want to know "what's wrong?" My answer is usually that "nothing is wrong" and that they need only keep steadily applying the instructions. Certainly, one doesn't become a proficient typist, musician, actor or sportsman because he has mastered the basic techniques. It takes time to acquire proficiency.

Let me assure you that anyone using and applying this technique can benefit from it. One of the troubles in dealing with any problem is routing defeatism and hopelessness. You can incorporate posthypnotic corrective measures in the suggestions that you give yourself. However, I believe that they must be dealt with on a conscious level as well. You must believe that you can conquer your difficulties no matter how long you have had them. If you are prepared to work with self-hypnosis in an unremitting manner, you will achieve the self-help that you seek. Now and then, you can anticipate a setback in your progress, but this needn't discourage you from your overall task. Recount the progress already made. If you have a "letdown" because you expected quicker and more dramatic results, remember that this is a common feeling shared by many with emotional problems. Remember, also, how long you have had the problem.

No doubt, you have tried other methods and became discouraged because you weren't making the progress you had anticipated. You dropped the idea and landed back where you started. Make up your mind, consciously, that you will work with untiring sincerity and a perseverance that will not falter because your chosen goal is not achieved immediately. I know of no therapy that leads straight to positive results without obstacles and intermittent failure. Success comes in spite of intervening failures because the ultimate direction has been clearly thought out and charted. Self-hypnosis will finally work because you are constantly conditioning your subconscious to react in a positive, constructive manner. The program must, of necessity, become automatic in nature. When it does, you will suddenly find yourself feeling the way you wanted to and doing the things that you set out to do with the aid of self-hypnosis. You actually cultivate those feelings that you want.

Hypnosis will not work with skeptics. Every so often such a person comes to my office seeking help. He tells me that his family physician or his spouse feels he should take my course in self-hypnosis. I inquire if he feels he might benefit from the course. If his answer is not positive, and if after talking to him at length about the benefits of hypnosis, I still feel he is not ready for the course, I suggest another mode of treatment for him. The reason for this is that unless the person is optimistic and enthusiastic about self-hypnosis, it just isn't going to work as effectively as it would otherwise. The very nature of a skeptical attitude limits the constructive forces that we wish to harness.

Occasionally, individuals want indisputable proof that hypnosis is going to help them. It is impossible to give them the proof and unqualified reassurance that they seek. Yet, these same people do not require proof from their physicians. No one can guarantee success. However, I do point out that the continued and intelligent use of self-hypnosis can be instrumental in directing the healing, curative, constructive forces of nature.

Many times, a metaphysical rather than a scientific approach is required. It's a matter of trying to satisfy the patient's needs. At times, it is helpful to allow the patient to attend a class in self-hypnosis. Being able to communicate and identify with other individuals seeking self-hypnosis often is enough to change his attitude. This is especially true when one or more of the students relates dramatic changes.

Self-hypnosis works because we are able to condition ourselves to various stimuli. We condition ourselves consciously and unconsciously to many activities. When we experience anxiety, it stems from a conditioning process which could have been conscious or unconscious. In self-hypnosis, the individual consciously works toward implementing and strengthening his own inherent strength and resources. These objectives, when attained, result in feelings of confidence, relaxation, self-mastery and well-being.

Furthermore, hypnosis utilizes a natural mental process. We all know that placebos work admirably in numerous cases. The dictionary defines the word placebo as, "an inactive substance or preparation, administered to please or gratify a patient, also used in controlled studies to determine the efficiency of medicinal substances." Many controlled experiments have shown that people achieve similar results whether they take a placebo (which they think is the real medication) or real medication that was prescribed. Several years ago many such tests were carried out with antihistamines to prevent colds. The results were always the same.

We are interested in what makes the placebo act as effectively as the true medication. It stands to reason that a chain reaction is set up, actually causing a physiological result from a psychological reaction. The unsuspecting patient declares, "I've never felt so good in my life." Yet, this would never have happened if he didn't think he was taking the marvelous new medicine. A recent scientific study by one of the leading pharmaceutical houses concluded that one third of the effectiveness of any medication depends upon the faith and trust that the patient has in the prescribing physician.

I am sure that the placebo results and the patient's faith in the physician as contributing factors to the effectiveness of medications do not come as a revelation. We are all aware of such information. Our problem is how to harness this unconscious process for constructive goals. The answer is through self-hypnosis.

Self-hypnosis, as we have explained it, uses a technique called visual-imagery. This has been referred to by many different names, but for our purposes we'll call it visual-imagery. Within this technique lies one of the keys for achieving the goals that you want. There have been many famous books written incorporating this technique as a basis for achievement. Perhaps the most famous of all is called *Think and Grow Rich* by Napoleon Hill. In recent years, *The Magic of Believing* by Claude M. Bristol and *The Power of Positive Thinking,* already mentioned, have become well-known. The book which gives direction to most of the books in this field is called *Self-Mastery Through Conscious Auto-Suggestion* by Dr. Emile Coué. I am sure the older readers of this book have heard of his famous saying, which I will repeat here for emphasis. "Day by day, in every way, I am getting better and better." Invariably, in all these books, there is reference to the Biblical quotation, "As a man thinketh in his heart, so is he."

As the reader can deduce, we are not theorizing about a startling new discovery. The technique is as ancient as man himself and his dream of a better tomorrow. All books using the visual-imagery technique tell you to paint a vivid, mental picture of the material things you wish to acquire, if it is a case of material wealth. For personal improvement, they tell you to paint a vivid picture of the individual you want to be. In most cases, you are told to do this in a relaxed or meditative state with as few distractions as possible. The next two requirements are constant repetition (conditioning) and a "burning desire" (motivation) to achieve what you set out to do.

Aren't these books really talking about self-hypnosis? Aren't they describing precisely the techniques of self-hypnosis? The terminology is different, but the approach is the same. With these techniques there is an aim to direct thinking, picturization, positive thinking, suggestions and constructive thoughts or images to the "inner self" or "real self." Aren't they once again really talking about the subconscious mind? I have no argument with any workable approach to emotional maturity, but in many cases we are actually becoming involved with the meaning of words (semantics). The quickest way to the subconscious is through self-hypnosis. In this self-hypnotic state, you are able to consciously direct suggestions to your subconscious mind.

Chapter 5

How to Arouse Yourself from the Self-Hypnotic State

You will note that this chapter precedes instruction on how to attain self-hypnosis. The reason for this is to alleviate whatever anxiety you may have in regard to the question, "If I'm hypnotized, how do I awaken myself?" It is important to understand that even though you are hypnotized, you are in control, are aware of your surroundings, what is going on about you, can think clearly and can arouse yourself very easily. It is only necessary to say or think, "I shall now open my eyes and wake up feeling fine." You could also give yourself a specific count and say, "As I count to five, I'll open my eyes and wake up feeling wonderfully well and refreshed. One . . . two . . . three . . . four . . . five."

It should be remembered that while we sometimes use the word "sleep" to describe the hypnotic state, we are not actually referring to true sleep. This accounts for much of the confusion. The individual thinks, "If I'm asleep, how can I awaken myself?" If the subject were asleep in the true sense of the word, this would be impossible. Actually, the subject is in a special or heightened state of awareness. In self-hypnosis, he is extremely conscious although his general physical appearance is one of passiveness. In the self-hypnotic state, the individual consciously gives himself whatever suggestions he desires. This proves he *is* conscious and, therefore, can awaken himself with the appropriate suggestions.

Occasionally, the subject falls asleep while giving himself suggestions or while relaxing to get into the right psychological mood. Naturally, in this case, the subject will awaken in due course. If the subject practices hypnosis when he is normally set to fall asleep in bed, he would awaken refreshed in the morning at his usual time.

Before beginning to give yourself therapeutic suggestions, you could give yourself the following suggestions which give you a *specific length of time* that you will work with self-hypnosis:

"I shall work with self-hypnosis for 15 minutes. At the end of that time, I shall open my eyes and wake up feeling wonderfully well, wide awake, confident, cheerful and optimistic. The moment I open my eyes, I'll feel refreshed. In case of any outside danger, I'll be able to awaken immediately, be fully alert and act accordingly."

You will notice that these suggestions take into consideration the possibility of something happening of danger to the individual, such as fire, etc. These points arise in the minds of most individuals attempting self-hypnosis and are well taken. You could also set an alarm clock to awaken you at a designated time.

Let us assume to arouse yourself you gave yourself a suggestion to open your eyes and be wide awake at the count of five. You count to five and for some reason you are unable to open your eyes. First of all, DON'T WORRY. Remain relaxed and give yourself the suggestions over again, emphasizing to yourself that at the count of five you will absolutely, positively be able to open your eyes very easily and will feel fine. You then begin the count again reiterating between each number that you will positively open your eyes at the count of five and be wide awake. This should do it. Should this not do it, may I reassure you again, DON'T BECOME ALARMED. Relax for a few minutes and try again. You'll be able to open your eyes and wake up.

I hope I haven't frightened you with the prospect of not being able to awaken. I bring this up only to acquaint you with the procedure to use. Actually, the problem of dehypnotization is a rare one. I should point out a very important fact. *I have never had a subject practicing or using self-hypnosis tell me he had the least bit of difficulty in awakening himself from the self-induced hypnotic state.*

I have had persons tell me that they heard or read of a case where the hypnotist could not bring the subject out of the hypnotic state, and, as a result, the subject slept for so many days. Not one of the stories could be documented. Years ago, for publicity purposes, stage hypnotists would have a subject sleep in a store window for several days. This was on a voluntary basis, though, and should not be confused with what we are discussing.

In working with subjects, I have *very rarely* had a subject who did not awaken at a specific count, but I have had this experience. I have usually found that the subject is so relaxed that he just didn't want to awaken for fear of losing this pleasant sensation. When the subject doesn't awaken, I merely ask him in a calm manner, "Why don't you wish to wake up? You can answer me without awakening from the hypnotic state." He usually replies he'd like to remain in this state for another five minutes or so. I agree to this extended period while getting a firm commitment from him that he will awaken after this period. This is usually sufficient to bring the subject out of the hypnotic state.

Occasionally, the instructions to wake up are not clear to the subject. If this is the case, clearer instructions should be given. You could also deepen the hypnotic state and then give suggestions to awaken at a specific count in a very authoritarian manner. Every so often, I have found that the subject has fallen into a natural sleep and just hasn't heard the instructions. In this case I raise my voice which is usually sufficient or gently shake the subject awakening him as you would any sleeping person.

I would like to relate a rather interesting experience that I had with a male subject. I had worked with this particular subject six times previous to this occasion. He was a good hypnotic subject, and he failed to awaken in the usual manner. Since he had carried out several post-hypnotic suggestions, it was rather perplexing to analyze what had happened. After about ten minutes, he finally agreed while he was under hypnosis to awaken at a given count. I asked him what was the nature of the difficulty. He replied, "I wanted to see how you would react."

In conclusion, having difficulty in dehypnotizing yourself is extremely rare. Should it happen, *keep calm,* and repeat the suggestions with emphasis. Even in hetero-hypnosis, where the hypnotist hypnotizes a subject, it is extremely rare. There are explainable psychodynamic factors for this. However, they can be met adequately while the subject is under hypnosis.

Chapter 6

How to Attain Self-Hypnosis

Let us begin with the hypothesis that anyone can learn and practice, to some degree, the science of self-hypnosis. We shall assume that you have carefully thought out what you want to accomplish. You have, through self-analysis, come up with reasonable goals of therapy and self-improvement. The next step is the acquisition of the hypnotic state, per se.

Before giving you the specific instructions, I would like to clarify a question which invariably arises in teaching a student self-hypnosis. It is: "Are the suggestions that I give myself as effective as the ones you would give me in hetero-hypnosis?"

It is natural to assume that the suggestions of the hypnotist would be more effective than those given by the subject himself, but both have the same intrinsic value. It is well to remember that all hypnosis is really self-hypnosis, and all hetero-suggestions are transposed into self-suggestions. If the hypnotist firmly suggests, "From this moment, you will feel very confident in all life situations," the subject automatically and unconsciously rephrases the statement, "From this moment, I will feel very confident in all life situations." The subject, ordinarily, mentally or aloud, repeats all suggestions using the pronoun "I" instead of "you."

The easiest and quickest way to learn self-hypnosis is to be hypnotized and given a posthypnotic suggestion to the effect that you will be able to put yourself into the hypnotic state at a given stimulus whenever you desire to do so. The hypnotist need not be a professional. Anyone understanding the rudiments of hypnosis can do this. However, let us assume you want to learn self-hypnosis and cannot find help. If you understand and consciously practice the instructions that I shall outline, you will attain your goal.

Sit in an easy chair or recline on a sofa or bed. Next, choose a point of eye fixation on the ceiling, preferably a spot behind you which would normally cause eye fatigue or strain. Now, breathe very slowly and deeply. As you do this, repeat, aloud or mentally, the word "sleep" as you inhale and "deep sleep" as you exhale. Do this for several minutes in a very monotonous manner until such time as you find yourself getting drowsy. Next, suggest to yourself that your eyelids are becoming heavy and tired. The goal is to acquire eye closure using this method. You want to reach a state where it is uncomfortable to keep the eyes open. Once you get your eyes closing, seemingly of their own volition, you have reached the first step in achieving self-hypnosis.

You can repeat to yourself such suggestions as, "My eyelids are becoming very heavy and tired... My eyes are becoming very watery... My eyelids are blinking... I just want to close my eyes ... The moment I close my eyelids, I shall fall into a deep, sound, hypnotic sleep ... Even though in a deep state of hypnosis, I shall be aware of my surroundings and be able to direct posthypnotic suggestions to my subconscious mind."

When your eyelids actually become heavy or when your eyes actually begin to water, you intensify these feelings by repeating affirmative suggestions along these very lines. This is known as "the feed-back technique" and helps to reinforce the actual condition that exists. Proceeding in this way hastens the actual closing of the eyes and attainment of the hypnotic state, per se.

Let us assume that you practice this procedure and seemingly nothing happens. Continue to practice it again and again until such time as you are able to achieve an eye closure. You will eventually be able to do this within a relatively short period of time.

One of the best times to practice the technique just given is when you are falling asleep at night. The lights are out and you are lying in bed. Choose an imaginary spot above and behind your eye level so there is some strain on the eye muscles. Now begin giving yourself suggestions that your eyelids are becoming heavy, etc.

The reason this period is such an excellent time to practice self-hypnosis is that the suggestions you give yourself spill over into your subconscious as you drift from consciousness to unconsciousness. It's like telling yourself to wake up at a certain time in the morning. The suggestion reaches your subconscious and activates you consciously to waken. Using this approach, you can give yourself dynamic, constructive suggestions at this time as well as giving yourself the posthypnotic suggestion that the next time you practice self-hypnosis, you will fall into a deeper, sound, hypnotic state at the count of three. You also emphasize that your eyelids will close involuntarily whenever you relax for five minutes and afterwards count to three. This conditioning process will be augmented by the use of the sleep period. The suggestions will tend to work unconsciously during this period and hasten your attainment of the constructive goals as well as the self-hypnotic goal itself.

Once you have achieved eye closure, deepen the hypnotic state by the following suggestions: "As I count to three, I shall go deeper and deeper into a profound, hypnotic state. As I count to three, I shall find myself becoming more and more relaxed. As I count to three, I shall fall into a deep, hypnotic sleep." You repeat these suggestions many times, actually trying on a conscious level to feel sleepier, more relaxed, more at ease. In doing this, you take on the characteristics of a deeply hypnotized subject.

Part of the difficulty in learning self-hypnosis is that the subject is aiming at a state of mind in which he has no experience. If I say, "Act happy" or "Act sad," there is an immediate reaction from your experiential background, and you can react accordingly. If you have never seen anyone hypnotized and I say, "Act as though you were hypnotized," you must, of necessity, act in a manner that you would assume approximated that of hypnosis. If you had actually seen someone hypnotized, you would naturally take on the characteristics you had observed. This would either be done consciously or unconsciously.

Some individuals describe the hypnotic state as a state of "complete relaxation." Many get a feeling of "detachment;" others a feeling of "disassociation," as though their entire being was only thought. Some get a "floating" or "drifting" feeling, likening the experience to lying on deep clouds. Others experience a heavy, pleasant, "sinking" feeling. Still others get a feeling of "peace and serenity." Many describe the hypnotic state as being akin to the state just prior to falling asleep or like daydreaming, and they experience the same reactions. Yet, there are some who do not feel a definite change. They describe it by saying, "I just felt that I had my eyes closed. I heard everything and was completely aware at all times." Since it is possible to direct your feelings (reactions), I would suggest that you aim for a completely relaxed, comfortable state.

You have now reached the point where your eyes are closed, and you have given yourself further suggestions to deepen the state of hypnosis. This has taken from about six to ten minutes. You are not sure, though, that you are under hypnosis. There are many ways to test this, and I shall outline one of these tests later in this chapter; however, for your initial attempts, it isn't too important whether or not you are under hypnosis. You are still to give yourself the posthypnotic suggestion that the next time you attempt to hypnotize yourself you will fall into a deeper and sounder state after you have relaxed for about five minutes and counted to three.

In your initial attempts, you will be trying to establish a conditioned response to the count of three which will subsequently cause your eyes to close and put you under hypnosis. Eventually, you should react instantly to the count of three or any other cue you may use to trigger the response. The key words or stimulus become associated with the action that you seek. Through repetition, just thinking about the stimulus can bring on the response. This is known as ideomotor action and is present in the waking as well as the hypnotic state. Pavlov's famous experiments which induced dogs to salivate when a bell was rung after previously having had food fed to them at the same time are examples of this type of conditioning. Don't we generally become hungry if someone tells us it's noon and time for lunch when, in fact, it's only 11 o'clock?

I had a common experience recently that I am sure many readers have shared. One of my neighbors, seeing my car was parked in front of my house and knowing I was home, called to say he was dropping in to see me. While working on the manuscript of this book, I thought I heard the doorbell as I was typing. I went to the front door and no one was there. I even walked around the house looking for him because I was so certain I heard the bell. This is another example of an ideomotor action. I told my friend about it when he arrived approximately 30 minutes later. He looked at me rather whimsically, and we both shared a laugh. Haven't you thought you heard the phone ring when you were waiting for a call?

In the chapter, "How Does Self-Hypnosis Work," stress was laid on the importance of the visual-imagery technique. During every attempt to achieve self-hypnosis, you attempt to visualize yourself going into the hypnotic state. Once you have deepened the state, you begin the process of visualizing yourself exactly the way you want to be. You may experience difficulty at first, but as you keep at it, you will be able to picture yourself the way you want. *You use the visual-imagery technique whether you think you are under hypnosis or not.* These images become clear as you constantly hammer home these suggestions. This is the exact procedure necessary, and you needn't complicate it.

Let us suppose that you are getting your eyelids to close at the count of three and have achieved a good state of relaxation. With these prerequisites, you can anticipate going deeper into the hypnotic state. Actually, being able to get the eyes to close at a specific count is the first test in determining if the subject has gone under hypnosis. If you have conditioned yourself this far, then you can go to the next step. The next test is called the "swallowing" test. You mentally give yourself suggestions that as you slowly, to yourself, count to 10, you will get an irresistible urge to swallow one time. You further suggest that this will happen even before you reach the count of 10. You then begin the count. "One... My throat is parched, and I feel an irresistible urge to swallow one time. Two... My lips are becoming very dry, and I feel an irresistible urge to swallow. Three... My throat feels very dry, and I feel an irresistable urge to swallow one time. Four... Before I reach the count of 10, the urge to swallow one time will become irresistible because my lips and throat are so dry. Five... Once I swallow, I shall no longer have the urge to swallow again, and as I swallow one time, I shall fall into a deeper and sounder state of hypnosis." Continue with similar suggestions, repeating and affirming the suggestions about swallowing. Once you actually swallow, you discontinue the suggestions and, instead, give yourself suggestions that you are falling deeper and deeper into a sound hypnotic state and that the constructive suggestions you now give yourself will work for you. Once again you practice visual-imagery, seeing yourself the way you want to be, while fortifying this image with forceful, positive suggestions. You close by giving yourself suggestions that you will enter the hypnotic state whenever you relax for five minutes and count to three.

The suggestions are just as effective whether given aloud or mentally. Many subjects report that they are reluctant when it comes to giving suggestions to themselves. I can only say that as you continue to work with yourself, you will develop confidence in giving yourself suggestions. In order for the suggestions to be effective, they cannot be given in a reticent or hesitant manner. They must be given with enthusiasm and anticipation. If you assiduously follow these instructions, you will derive the benefits you seek in the shortest possible time and witness the positive, tangible results of your suggestions and efforts. In the next chapter, you'll learn how to deepen the self-hypnotic state.

Chapter 7

Deepening the Self-Hypnotic State

For each progressive test, it is usually necessary to have accomplished the preceding tests. However, this is not an absolute rule. Frequently, a subject responds to tests at the beginning of the depth scale and then to others at the end of the depth scale. Certain tests in between do not work. I have had the following experience more than once while teaching one of my classes in self-hypnosis. In testing the depth of hypnosis, I run the gamut of all of the tests from light to deep. In this way, the subject can ascertain how far he has progressed. One frequent test for the deep state is to give the subject a posthypnotic suggestion to the effect that the next cigarette he smokes will have a vile taste and it will be absolutely impossible for him to take more than three puffs. It is further suggested that after the third puff, the cigarette taste will be so unbearable it will become necessary for him to extinguish the cigarette.

We can expect an excellent hypnotic subject to comply with these posthypnotic suggestions, but a subject who hasn't even passed the eye closure test (test No. 1) or any other test may unexpectedly react perfectly to the cigarette test which we know is a standard test for determining if the subject has entered into a deep state of hypnosis. How can you account for it? There is no simple or positive answer. If we hadn't given him this particular test, he would have felt that he wasn't making progress in his determination to become a good hypnotic subject. Because of this, he might not have given himself therapeutic suggestions because he would feel he hadn't reached a state of hypnosis which would benefit him. Remember, follow the instructions of giving yourself whatever therapeutic suggestions you want, regardless of the fact that you feel that "nothing has happened." I have seen many subjects who were bewildered because certain tests did not work, yet were pleased because of very gratifying overall results from using self-hypnosis. They were baffled because of their inability to pass certain tests which they felt were a prerequisite to the success of constructive suggestions they gave themselves.

It is commonly felt that the deeper the state of hypnosis, the better the results. In actual practice, I have not found this to be so. I have had excellent results in a relatively short period of time with subjects who only achieved a light state, and it has been necessary to work with others who achieved a deep state of hypnosis for a longer period before lasting results were in evidence. Naturally, each individual presents a different set of needs and even though the symptoms may be basically the same, each will respond favorably when his requirements are met. This happens on a conscious as well as unconscious level. For example, the mere assurance by a physician that the patient is all right and has nothing to worry about is often sufficient to bring about desirable results. Another example is the mother who stops the sobbing of her hurt child by a loving kiss. A logical approach, pointing out to the child that he really didn't hurt himself, would never have worked. We have all heard stories of primitive tribesmen who have died because they knew they were the objects of "death wishes" by another member of the tribe.

The key to achieving a greater depth of self-hypnosis lies in the use of the visual-imagery technique. You "see" yourself going into the hypnotic state deeper and deeper. You even picture yourself, using this technique, passing various progressive hypnotic tests. The second part of the key lies in giving yourself a posthypnotic suggestion that each succeeding attempt will put you into a deeper state as a result of a given stimulus—such as the count of three.

The following instructions should not be attempted usually unless you have been successful in achieving the two basic tests — the eye closure as well as the uncontrollable urge to swallow followed by the physical act of swallowing at a specific count. If the conditioning process works for these two tests, you have achieved the lethargic state of hypnosis. This is the first state of hypnosis and is generally referred to as the "light" state. Therapeutic suggestions can work admirably in this state. The next stage of hypnosis is known as the cataleptic state and is referred to as the "medium" state. Generally, hypnosis is divided into three states: the lethargic (light state); the cataleptic (medium state); and the somnambulistic (deep state).

As you deepen the hypnotic state, you can accomplish the progressive tests that I shall outline for you. I'll also number these tests for the convenience of having a reference. Deepening the hypnotic state requires the same type of practice or conditioning as the first two steps. Let us call eye closure—No. 1, and swallowing—No. 2. We are now ready to proceed to the "hand tingling" test—No. 3.

You have just completed tests No. 1 and 2; you are in a completely relaxed state. Now give yourself the following suggestions: "As I count to ten and even before I reach the count of ten, I shall feel a light tingling or numb feeling in my right hand." As you slowly begin the count of ten, you keep repeating suggestions to the effect that your right hand is beginning to tingle. Once again, you practice the technique of visual-imagery, tapping your experiential background for this feeling. You can recall how it feels when your hand goes to sleep. Once you get an initial feeling of lightness, tingling or numbness, reinforce this feeling by the feed-back technique as you did with the eye closure test. As you practice this procedure, it will work with greater effectiveness. The following is a very important point to remember. Be sure that you give yourself a posthypnotic suggestion that the tingling, light or numb sensation will disappear as you continue to count to 15. For example, "As I count to 15, the tingling feeling in my right hand will disappear, and I shall experience only normal sensations. Eleven... The tingling feeling is leaving. Twelve... Now it is leaving faster. Thirteen... I can feel my hand returning to normal. Fourteen... The tingling feeling has left. Fifteen... My right hand feels perfectly normal." You could try a variation of this test by saying your nose or one of your toes will itch at a specific count. Once this test is accomplished, you are ready for the "foot" test—No. 4.

You will remember that the key to achieving a greater depth of hypnosis lies in visualizing yourself going deeper with each attempt and accomplishing progressive hypnotic tests. Keep this in mind. For a moment, let us go back to the hand tingling test—No. 3. Once you have been successful in accomplishing this test, use the visual-imagery technique to see yourself successfully responding to the foot test. When you have actually accomplished test No. 4, you see yourself accomplishing the "hand levitation" test—No. 5. In other words, you use each step to enhance a greater receptivity for the following progressive test. As you couple this approach with posthypnotic suggestions that you will go deeper and deeper into the hypnotic state at a given stimulus, you set into motion a conditioned response mechanism which must ultimately guide you into a profound state of hypnosis.

The foot test can be accomplished while sitting or lying down. The idea of this test is to imagine that your feet are stuck to the floor or that your legs are so heavy that they are impossible to raise until you reach a certain count. It is best to begin this test by trying to capture a heavy, relaxed feeling in your legs. You give yourself specific suggestions along these lines: "As I count to five, I shall notice a very heavy, relaxed, pleasant feeling in both legs. It will be a very comfortable feeling; a feeling of complete relaxation." You then begin the count of ten, following out the idea of the other tests you have successfully accomplished. You should remember that there is no time limit and you take as much time as you need in order to get the relaxed, heavy feeling. Once you get the relaxed, heavy feeling, you use the visual-imagery technique to try to picture your legs stuck to the floor. If you are lying down, imagine you are covered by a heavy blanket which is tightly tucked under the mattress, making it impossible for you to raise your legs. If sitting up, I tell the subject to imagine that his shoes are stuck to the floor with "iron glue," and since his feet are in the shoes, it is impossible to lift them until the specific count which will enable him to do so.

Here are the suggestions you can use for the second part of this test. "As I continue to count to ten, I shall find that it will be impossible for me to raise my legs. I shall try at the count of ten, but it will be absolutely impossible to raise my legs until I count to 15. At that time, I shall be able to raise my legs easily, and the heavy feeling will leave as well." You then continue with the count, giving yourself appropriate suggestions. Once this test is accomplished, you use the visual-imagery technique to see yourself accomplishing the hand levitation test—No. 5. Be sure you give yourself the posthypnotic suggestion that the next time you hypnotize yourself, you will fall into a deeper and sounder state.

I'll assume that you have been able to get a relaxed, heavy feeling in your legs. You have reached the count of five and are ready to proceed further. Here are sample suggestions you can use: "Six . . . My legs are becoming extremely heavy. Seven . . . I'll be unable to lift them until I count to 15. Eight . . . I feel very comfortable; my legs are becoming heavier and heavier. Nine . . . My entire body is completely relaxed, and my legs are so heavy that they are impossible to lift. Ten . . . I'm in a very deep hypnotic state, and it is absolutely impossible for me to move my legs until I count to 15." At this point, you actually try to raise your legs. If you can't do it, you have reached the cataleptic stage.

Should you not be able to raise your legs, don't become frightened. All you need to say is: "I can now move my legs." You could also say: "As I count to three, I'll be able to move my legs." However, since we have elected originally to be able to move the legs at the count of 15, it would be best to follow out this pattern. You could at this time merely continue to count to 15, at which time you would be able to move your legs. I prefer giving suggestions between each count as follows: "Eleven... The heavy feeling is leaving, and I shall be able to raise my legs at the count of 15. Twelve... I can feel the heavy, relaxed feeling leaving. Thirteen... I am beginning to move my legs. Fourteen... I am lifting my legs more and more. Fifteen... I have perfect control over my bodily functions and legs; I am lifting and moving my legs; the heavy feeling is dissipating; I am in complete control; I can now give myself posthypnotic suggestions that will be very effective and beneficial." Give yourself whatever suggestions you want at this time.

Let us suppose that you tried the foot test for some time and were unsuccessful. Perhaps this puzzles you, and you wonder why it didn't work. Perhaps you were able to get a heavy feeling in the legs, but the second part of the test didn't work. The following information will help you to understand why you were unable to complete this cataleptic test. Either you had not conditioned yourself sufficiently, or you weren't really "letting go" enough to enter into a deeper state of hypnosis. Most subjects need to test themselves and feel secure every step of the way. They don't just plunge into the cataleptic or somnambulistic stages immediately. In this connection, I believe it can be compared with the bather who goes into the water one step at a time. Even the playful splashing directed at him by friends does not compel him to duck under the water. Instead, he continues to slowly go deeper and deeper until he is completely submerged. Wouldn't it have been easier to duck under all at once? Perhaps, but I'm sure you have either experienced the same thing yourself or seen it happen.

The analogy should be clear. The subject is reluctant to do what he considers as "giving up his control" when, in reality, he is really more and more in control of himself as he penetrates the deeper levels of hypnosis.

In reality, the subject who does not or cannot raise his feet really could move in case of emergency, even without counting to 15. He has, in effect, entered into a state in which it is too much bother to lift his feet. A common example of this frame of mind is when you remain in bed in the morning even though you know you will be late to work. You are just too comfortable to move, and your initiative seems paralyzed.

Let us assume, at this point, that you have finally succeeded in getting the foot test to work. You are now ready for the hand levitation test—No. 5. In this test, the goal is to get your hand to slowly rise and touch your chin. Once it touches your chin, you enter into a still deeper state and lower your hand slowly to your side. This test is actually combined with the hand tingling test—No. 3. Since you have been successful with test No. 3, the rest is rather simple. This time as you work test No. 3, aim for a light, pleasant feeling in your right hand. Once you get this reaction, you give yourself suggestions that your right hand will now rise and touch your chin. As soon as it does, you will fall into a deeper state and lower your hand. Here are the suggestions that you can use: "As I count to ten and even before I reach the count of ten, I shall have an irresistible impulse to slowly raise my hand to my chin. As I progress with the counting, my hand will slowly rise, and the impulse will become stronger and stronger. As soon as my hand touches my chin, the impulse will leave. I will then lower my hand and fall into a very deep hypnotic state. I shall be fully aware of what is happening, my surroundings, and will be able to give myself beneficial posthypnotic suggestions."

At this point you start counting to ten, giving yourself suggestions that your right hand which already has a light feeling will begin to slowly rise to your chin. Time the counting to coincide with the actual physical act of raising your hand. You are trying to feel an involuntary urge to raise your hand. The movement itself should also be of an unconscious rather than conscious nature. A conscious raising of your hand to your chin is not what you are looking for in this test. Should you experience difficulty in attaining the first movement of your hand, you can give yourself assistance by consciously and slowly raising your hand just to get it started. The rest of the movement, as mentioned, must be automatic. Should you find it necessary to start your hand rising, use the feed-back technique to continue the movement. You can give yourself the following suggestions:

"One... my right hand is beginning to rise Two... My right hand is very, very light, and I am getting an irresistible urge to slowly raise it. Three... This feeling is getting stronger and stronger. Four... My right hand is rising more and more. Five... My hand is rising toward my chin. Six... As soon as my hand touches my chin, I shall fall into a deeper and sounder state of hypnosis. Seven... My hand is rising closer and closer toward my chin. Eight... The feeling of lightness is becoming stronger and stronger. Nine... My right hand is about to touch my chin; as soon as it does, I'll fall into a very deep hypnotic state. Ten... My right hand is touching my chin; I'm falling deeper and deeper into a sound hypnotic state; I'll now slowly lower my hand and continue falling into a deep, sound, pleasant state of hypnosis. The light feeling has left my hand."

You should not attempt to memorize the exact phraseology for any of the tests. You are to merely use the suggestions that have been written out for you as a guide. The timing of the suggestions is the paramount consideration in attaining successful results. Don't be impatient. Take as much time as you need. Should you find yourself unsuccessful after ten or fifteen minutes, drop the test and come back to it another day. I haven't found that working at a specific test all day long accomplishes the end result.

It is best to work for a specific period every day. In this way, the conditioned response pattern is established for the success of the tests as well as the success of the post-hypnotic suggestions that you have given yourself. You should bear in mind that if you have been successful in achieving the first five tests, you have reached a medium state of hypnosis, and posthypnotic suggestions will be extremely effective. In the next chapter, you'll learn, psychologically, how to go even deeper into hypnosis. You'll learn those psychological factors that are important to know and that can contribute to your development into an excellent hypnotic subject. Following this, the subsequent chapter will give you further tests and instructions for developing into a somnambulistic subject.

Chapter 8

What You Should Know About Becoming An Excellent Subject

Becoming an excellent subject follows the same general rules for becoming proficient in any other endeavor. It depends upon your motivation, persistence and willingness to devote time and study to the subject. Let us agree that most individuals can learn to play a musical instrument to some degree. This degree is usually sufficient for their own needs. To become a virtuoso, however, it is necessary to study the instrument and devote a great deal of energy and time to practice. The same example could be given for most undertakings. Anyone can learn to hit a golf ball, but being able to control the direction and distance and become a skilled golfer is quite another matter.

If you have been successful in accomplishing the first five tests, you can consider yourself a good hypnotic subject. Becoming an excellent subject entails following the same procedure used in accomplishing the first five tests. Some may proceed very easily into the somnambulistic state, and others may have a difficult time reaching this deepest stage. Understanding some of the psychology involved and assuming the right psychological frame of mind for the attainment of the somnambulistic state is more important than just working blindly in an attempt to get the somnambulistic tests to work. Being irritable, disgusted and despondent because of your inability to go further into hypnosis is not the answer and will only lead to frustration and failure. The reader is not to assume he will be a difficult subject. If you have come this far, you'll be able to continue in the same manner. The topic under discussion now is brought up to prepare readers for any contingency that may arise. It's like having a life preserver on a boat. You hope you never need it, but you should be prepared to use it in case of an emergency.

It is natural to assume that if you are willing and trying to go into the lethargic, cataleptic or somnambulistic state, you will be able to do so in a relatively short period of time. Unfortunately, this is by no means the case. Many of the principles of learning and conditioning can be applied to hypnosis, but with many subjects these laws do not seem applicable. Let us assume you wanted to learn to become an excellent typist. This is a reasonable goal and all that is necessary is to continue practicing until you have reached the proficiency you set out to achieve. This proficiency would, as a rule, follow application of the laws of learning and conditioning.

This isn't always so in a subject's attempt to become somnambulistic. When the subject progresses from one stage to another in a classical manner, the theory works admirably, but what happens when a subject cannot seem to progress any further? He has reached a plateau and is unable to climb higher. He seems to have reached a psychological impasse or stalemate. It is easy to say that the subject is thwarted by a subconscious block and let it go at that. This, however, doesn't help him in his dilemma. It's like telling the stranded motorist that the reason his car has stalled is because the motor isn't running. The following information will be helpful to those who haven't been able to reach the first stages of hypnosis, as well as those who apparently can go only so far. Actually, the same principles are involved.

If the subject doesn't respond or responds to a limited degree, there evidently is a cause or reason for this poor response. In order to continue this discussion, it will be necessary for us to agree that the resistance can be either conscious or unconscious. If the subject insists that he is trying to "let go," has nothing to hide, is not afraid of hypnosis, understands what is involved and has strong motivation, we can only assume that the resistance must be unconscious. Usually, it will be necessary to work through this unconscious resistance before the subject responds. If the subject is conditioning himself, this will involve a great deal of introspection, and even then it is an extremely difficult job. One doesn't usually have proper insight into one's own emotional make-up. The end result is that one can only rationalize about his behavior.

Let us explore some interesting aspects of hypnosis with a view toward helping you if you are having difficulty responding the way you desire. I have had the following paradoxical situation happen many times. A subject calls my office, requesting to be conditioned for self-hypnosis. He further requests that he be allowed to bring along a member of his family or a friend for the hypnotic session. These individuals usually ask if I object to this procedure. I interpreted this request as a sign of distrust during my early career as a professional hypnotist. I was affronted by the idea of the unspoken insinuation verbalized by this request. Didn't they trust me? Between trying to defend myself and assuring them that there was no need for another person being present, since my secretary could observe the procedure, I usually "won" the argument but lost the client. As I developed understanding into the needs of these persons, I began to realize that the request was not directed at my integrity, but was a safeguard for their ego.

Here is an interesting sidelight that has happened frequently in regard to the foregoing situation. I would request the subject to sit near my desk and tell the onlooker to sit in back and to the side of the subject, away from the subject's view so as not to distract him. In this situation, I invariably place the hypnodisc on a spinning, portable phonograph turntable and turn it upright for the subject to look at. The hypnodisc, which is made of stiff cardboard, looks like a 12-inch phonograph record and has concentric heavy lines drawn on it. As it spins, the subject feels he is being pulled toward the center. At the same time, it causes his eyes to become very tired. I have included a drawing of it on this page for those who are not familiar with this hypnotic device. The revolving hypno-

disc causes a physiological reaction and must work with everyone. You feed back certain known physiological responses for the successful attainment of hypnosis.

The onlooker has no choice but to look at the hypnodisc as well. As I suggest to the subject that his eyes are becoming heavy and tired and that soon he'll have an irresistible impulse to close them, the onlooker is naturally hearing the same suggestion. Because this person feels apart from the hypnotic situation, there can be no conscious resistance. Since these defenses are not hampering the attainment of hypnosis, the onlooker may readily fall under hypnosis. More than once, the onlooker has confided to me that he was getting a better night's sleep, was feeling wonderfully well or had derived other benefits since coming to my office as an "observer." The exact situation happens when the stage hypnotist is hypnotizing subjects on the stage. Many times a person in the audience who had no intention of becoming hypnotized becomes influenced in the same manner. Incidentially, these individuals make the best subjects.

There are interesting theories as to why a subject responds or docs not respond to hypnosis. I think the reader would find some of these theories interesting and perhaps gain some insight into his own hypnotic behavior. These theories are based primarily on a psychoanalytical approach to hypnosis.

The most prevalent theory is that the hypnotist represents either the father image (paternal or fear hypnosis) or the mother image (maternal or love hypnosis). The father usually represents an authoritarian figure. The subject's identification can be on a conscious or subconscious level. Let us suppose the subject has ambivalent feelings toward his father. Because of this, he may not respond. Here is an opportunity to frustrate the authoritative (father) figure. The only trouble with this theory is that if there is an excellent relationship between the father and subject, it doesn't necessarily mean that the subject will respond easily. The stage hypnotist invariably uses a strong, authoritative approach with a great deal of success, but this approach generally does not work best in private practice.

I have found that for the majority of subjects the maternal approach works best. Perhaps the process of hypnosis awakens early unconscious memories of being put to sleep as a child. Some techniques that are used in hypnosis are quite similar to this. The subject, who is lying down, is told to close his eyes and is spoken to in a quiet, reassuring, monotonous tone of voice. The hypnotist is seated near him. The hypnotist even uses the same words that the subject has heard as a child: "Sleep. Go to sleep. When you awaken, you'll feel wonderfully well." In fact, I use some special music that I had recorded for inducing hypnosis. The first musical selection is Brahms' "Lullaby." Children's music boxes invariably contain this selection, and the melody cannot help but activate a pleasant nostalgia. It is a memory associated with love and tenderness. This brings us to the fact that hypnosis may offer the subject a chance to escape from the reality of pressing problems into a state of complete irresponsibility. In fact, one theory of hypnosis equates the hypnotic state as a form of unconscious regression and need for submission.

The male subject may have a strong, positive identification with his mother rather than his father. It is part of the unresolved Oedipus complex. He sees his mother as a kind, loving individual, always ready to help. Even if the mother did something socially unacceptable, the individual would defend her vehemently. The father who might do something wrong would rarely be excused. Just the opposite is true with the female subject. When asking the female child, "Whose girl are you?", the answer is invariably, "Daddy's girl." When asking the male child, "Whose boy are you?", the answer is invariably, "Momma's boy." We accept this transference of identification as a normal process of growing up. When it isn't normally resolved, it can account for severe personality problems. One might assume, therefore, that a woman hypnotist could better hypnotize a male subject, and a male hypnotist could better hypnotize a female subject, but this is not true except for cases such as we have just mentioned.

One school of thought feels that there is a strong submissive tendency in all of us and hypnosis gratifies this wish. The individual's need for dependence is also met. In this case, the hypnotist becomes omnipotent, being able to alter feelings that ordinarily distress the individual. Normally, adults, when confronted by a particularly upsetting experience, might want to be held closely by an intimate friend or member of the family. Don't we frequently put our arm around a friend in grief trying to comfort him? The inner strength which is created by hypnosis within the total personality structure of the subject lessens dependency upon the hypnotist, much in the same fashion that we need the doctor less as we start to recover from an illness. Self-hypnosis further lessens dependency for no authoritarian figure is used.

The subject's attitude towards authority is important to know. It is well-known that officers in the army are more difficult to hypnotize than noncommissioned men. The enlisted man, by a process of indoctrination and conditioning, is taught to obey and follow orders without reasoning. The transference of authority to the hypnotist is readily accomplished because of this conditioning process. The army doctor, when treating patients psychologically, replaces his army jacket with a regular white medical jacket to increase rapport.

One interesting theory is that the subject responds as he thinks the hypnotist would like him to. This is termed "role playing." When asking a subject under hypnosis his name, you usually get a very slow, deliberate answer, as though the subject were in a trance. You tell him that he can answer in a normal speaking voice and tempo and his further replies are to be in the same manner as his waking state.

Another theory along these lines is that the subject acts as he believes a hypnotized person would act. This, too, is role playing, but it does not explain analgesia, such as when the dentist hypnotizes the patient and proceeds to drill a tooth. No one (with the possible exception of a highly neurotic psychic masochist) is going to endure excruciating pain just to please the doctor.

One theory about hypnosis states that it allows the subject an opportunity of identifying with the hypnotist, whom he sees as a powerful figure. Through this identification, the subject is able to gain inner strength. On the other hand, the subject might rebel against the submissive nature of the hypnotic setting. This could easily create anxiety which, in turn, could create hostility resulting in resistance of various kinds. As a result of this, the subject might begin to criticize the hypnotist, find fault with the way he (the subject) is being handled, question the judgment of the hypnotist, or doubt the effectiveness of the hypnotic procedure.

Many investigators assert that the "rapport," meaning the relationship between the subject and hypnotist, is all important. This is true and the relationship can and does have many ramifications. In psychotherapy, the term "transference" is used to denote this relationship. The relationship is further described as a good or bad transference. There is also a countertransference which indicates the reaction of the therapist to the patient. Naturally, in order for the subject to respond, there must be good rapport.

I have tried to indicate that there are complexities that may arise in the hypnotic setting. There are many conflicting theories as to why a subject does or does not respond. There are no set rules to follow, and one's intuition, experience and judgment help solve any problem that arises.

Let me relate another frequent incident. I have had subjects come to me after they were unable to be hypnotized by several other professional hypnotists. They have complained that the hypnotists weren't "good hypnotists" because they couldn't hypnotize them. After all, they ask, hadn't they been willing subjects? My usual answer is that the fault, if there is one, is not with the hypnotists and really not with the subjects. It is a matter of exploring what has happened and then deciding on a course of action to insure success.

I am firmly convinced that the subject responds when he is positively, without equivocation, ready to do so. He keeps testing the response to make sure he is in control. He fears a reduction in his voluntary level of reality attachment and control. Unresponsiveness proves to him that he has this control. As long as he does this, which is a natural response, he never lets go sufficiently to attain hypnosis. Hypnosis, as we know, is a very sensitive state. It requires complete faith and trust in the hypnotist. If it is lacking, the subject never does respond. The phenomenon of hypnosis is entirely subjective in nature, and its success lies within the total personality structure of the subject. If there is resistance to hypnosis itself or to deepening the state, the subject by his own honest evaluation and verbalization of his resistance can do much to become a better subject. Hypnosis must begin with the acceptance by the subject of certain basic fundamentals that we have already discussed rather than of the forcefulness of the hypnotist. The deepening of the hypnotic state lies in the intensification of the conditioned response mechanism once it has been initiated.

You should not expect to achieve immediate results although sometimes this does happen. As you continue to work with perseverance, intelligence and enthusiasm, you will definitely achieve the goals that you have set for yourself. It is well to remember that you guide yourself toward the somnambulistic state, depending upon your belief and acceptance of those principles that have been outlined for you.

I have attempted to point out some of the salient points and theories to keep in mind in your attempt to develop into an excellent hypnotic subject. Some of these only pertain to the situations where the hypnotist works with the subject. Many of the problems inherent in this setting are not applicable to the situation where the subject is hypnotizing himself. Both settings have their advantages and disadvantages. As long as you proceed to follow the instructions given you, you can feel assured that you will finally achieve self-hypnosis.

It should be emphasized that it is vital to adopt the right

frame of mind in your attempt to achieve self-hypnosis, particularly a deep state. If you approach hypnosis with a "prove-it-to-me" attitude, nothing is going to happen. Self-hypnosis requires practicing a set of mental exercises or mental gymnastics. To acquire the ultimate from this training requires systematic conditioning. The word "training" is used quite extensively in hypnotic literature. The use of the word implies that hypnosis can be attained by a training period. The literature speaks frequently of a subject being trained to respond in a certain way. Obviously, this means over a certain period of time. It also means you train yourself to become a good hypnotic subject. It is a skill that all can acquire.

There are four books dealing specifically with self-hypnosis that I would recommend to you for further reading. They are: *What is Hypnosis* by Andrew Salter, *Hypnosis and Self-Hypnosis* by Bernard Hollander, M.D., *Autogenic Training* by Johannes H. Schultz, M.D., and *Self-Hypnosis—Its Theory, Technique and Application* by Melvin Powers.

Chapter 9

Techniques for Reaching the Somnambulistic State

As indicated in the last chapter, the attainment of the somnambulistic stage of hypnosis can represent an extremely intricate procedure. Because of certain inherent characteristics of this stage, it is easier to attain by heterohypnosis. However, this does not preclude the fact that it can be reached without the aid of a hypnotist. More important than the testing and deepening procedures that I shall outline for you in this chapter are an *understanding* and an *awareness* of some of the complexities involved, first in achieving the hypnotic state, then deepening, and, finally, reaching somnambulism. There are no absolute or final answers to many of the problems that can arise. You can become entangled with rationalization so easily when you want the facts to fit a particular theory. I point this out to the reader because, as the subject goes deeper, the procedure can become more complicated.

There are many interesting phenomena which can be elicited in the somnambulistic state. They are of interest for the most part, to students of abnormal behavior and are pertinent from an academic viewpoint. They do not fall within the province of this book or of hypnosis for therapeutic purposes and might lead the reader astray. Should readers be interested in further hypnotic phenomena, I refer them to *Modern Hypnosis* by Leslie Kuhn and Salvadore Russo, Ph.D., *Experimental Hypnosis* by Leslie LeCron, *Time Distortion in Hypnosis* by Milton Erickson, M.D. and Lynn F. Cooper, M.D., and *Hypnotism—An Objective Study in Suggestibility* by André M. Weitzenhoffer, Ph.D.

As discussed previously, some individuals experience difficulty in attaining the deeper hypnotic states. My advice is to be patient and to continue working with yourself. It is not imperative or vital to reach the somnambulistic stage for therapeutic results. It is a misconception on the part of many students that they must go into the deepest state possible to obtain results. Dramatic changes can come about at all levels of hypnosis. The somnambulistic state is necessary in hypnotherapy when there is a need for the patient to relive some traumatic episode. It is also useful when the patient is reluctant to consciously discuss certain aspects of his problem. Many hypnotherapeutic techniques such as amnesia, hypermnesia, progression, paramnesia, automatic writing, dream induction, regression, production of experimental conflicts and crystal or mirror gazing require a somnambulistic state. For those of you interested in hypnotherapy, I can recommend no finer book than *Hypnotherapy of War Neuroses* by John G. Watkins, Ph.D. In this book, the theory of hypnotherapy has been diagramatically presented for easy comprehension and shown to be an amalgamation of concepts and practices from various schools of thought.

Most students of hypnosis equate the phenomenon of amnesia with the somnambulistic state. The mistake they make is in trying to achieve amnesia. It's similar to the dog trying to catch his tail. It is impossible for the subject to effectively suggest amnesia to himself. If he remembers what he was supposed to forget, he has failed. If he truly doesn't remember what he was supposed to forget, he doesn't even remember the amnesia suggestion and can take no satisfaction from his success because he is not aware that he has accomplished the posthypnotic suggestion. Unless an elaborate set of posthypnotic suggestions are worked out, it is an impossible test for self-hypnosis.

I know the reader is anxious to begin his conditioning for the somnambulistic state, but there are still a few pertinent remarks which should be remembered before proceeding further. The reader should not memorize verbatim any of the tests involved in proving the somnambulistic state. All that is necessary to remember is the general form and the goal you seek. The goal is to increase your suggestibility which, in turn, means deepening of the hypnotic state. After each step, you are to give yourself suggestions that you will go still deeper the next time. You should also designate a specific length of time to work with self-hypnosis. The suggestions are as follows: "I shall work with self-hypnosis for 15 minutes. At the end of that time, I shall open my eyes and wake up feeling wonderfully well. I'll be wide awake and refreshed. In case of any danger, I'll be able to awaken immediately and act accordingly."

Some hypnotists tell their subjects to "make your mind a blank." I suppose what they really mean is that you must try to think of only what the hypnotist is saying. Have you ever tried to make your mind a blank? Try it for a moment. It's an impossibility. Should the hypnotist persist along these lines, he'll never be successful. It is the wrong approach. The subject, because of his inability to comply with this suggestion, is fighting a losing battle. It is also almost impossible for the subject to concentrate only on what the hypnotist is saying. Any word the hypnotist says can start a conscious as well as unconscious train of thought. Therefore, in reality, this, too, is impossible. However, it really isn't necessary that the subject keep his thoughts concentrated solely on what is being said so long as they are kept in the general area. At times, the more you try to concentrate, the more your thoughts become scattered. Suppose I say to you, "Forget the address 8721 Sunset Boulevard." What happens? The more you try to forget it, the more you remember it. Therefore, don't be concerned if you experience stray thoughts during the induction and deepening of hypnosis. You are now ready to continue with further tests. The first five tests should be mastered before continuing.

Test No. 6 is referred to as the "fly" test. In this test, once under hypnosis, you picture that a fly is crawling on the back of your right or left hand. Once you feel the fly, you know you are deeply hypnotized. You might even get an urge to move your hand and flick the fly off your hand. When this happens, you know, of course, that you are deeply hypnotized. Here is a sample of the type of suggestions to give:

"As I count to ten and even before I reach the count of ten, I shall feel a fly crawling on the back of my right hand. This illusion will seem very real to me. One...My right hand is completely relaxed. Two ... I feel completely at ease. Three...I am beginning to feel a pleasant tingling feeling on the back of my right hand. Four...

This feeling is becoming strong. Five...It feels as though a fly is moving on the back of my hand. Six...I have had this same feeling before. Seven...I can feel the fly. Eight ...The feeling is very definite. Nine...As I flick my hand the fly will disappear (If you have felt the fly, move your hand). Ten...It is gone."

Test No. 7 is known as the "cigarette" test and naturally is only for those of you who smoke. In this test, you give yourself posthypnotic suggestions during the hypnotic state, awaken yourself, and then note the effects of the posthypnotic suggestions. If the cigarette tastes bitter or has a repugnant taste or odor, and if you furthermore find it impossible to smoke more than three puffs, necessitating your putting out the cigarette, you know the posthypnotic suggestions are working perfectly and that you are an excellent hypnotic subject. Here are the suggestions to give yourself while you are under hypnosis:

"When I count to three, I shall open my eyes and wake up feeling wonderfully well and shall have a strong desire to smoke a cigarette. Upon lighting the cigarette, I shall notice that there is a very bitter, strong and repugnant taste to the cigarette. As I continue to smoke the cigarette, the distasteful effect will become stronger and stronger. Even though I realize that I have given myself these post-hypnotic suggestions, they will exert a strong force outside of my conscious control, and I shall find it necessary to extinguish the cigarette after three puffs. As I now count to three, I shall open my eyes and wake up feeling fine. One, two, three."

Test No. 8 is called the "sun" test. In this test, you picture yourself in a bathing suit, shorts or playsuit at the beach or some other familiar place taking a sunbath. You imagine that it is a beautiful summer day. As you see yourself relaxed, you imagine that a cloud is blocking out the sun, but as you count to three, the cloud will move away and you will feel the warm, pleasant glow of the sun's rays on your face and hands. Here are the suggestions you can use:

"As I count to three, I shall feel the warm, pleasant rays of the sun on my face and hands. One...The cloud is moving, and I can begin to feel the warm, pleasant rays of the sun. Two...The cloud is moving more and more, exposing more and more of the sun. I can feel the warmth of the sun's rays. Three...The cloud has moved away from the sun, and I can feel the full, warm strength of the sun. It is a pleasant feeling, but as I continue to count to five, the warm feeling will dissipate. Four...The warm feeling is leaving. Five...The warm feeling has left, and I feel perfectly normal in every respect."

A variation of this test is to see yourself lying comfortably in front of a fireplace. In this instance, you imagine someone is adding wood to the fire. As this is done, you feel the warm glow of the fire more and more. Should you use the fireplace technique, try to incorporate the sound of rain into the picture. If you "hear" rain you have created a positive auditory hallucination and can consider yourself an excellent subject.

You can also visualize a situation where you would be cold. This is not as pleasant as the picture that one can conjure up about a fireplace and thus creates a bit more resistance since no one wants to feel uncomfortable.

Test No. 9 is the "breeze" test. It can be combined with the previous test. After you attain the feeling of warmth, you give yourself a count of three (or whatever number you want), suggesting that you will feel the cool ocean breeze (if you are at the beach) on your face and hands.

You can even carry this step further, suggesting that you'll even smell the odor of the salt water. This is known as an olfactory illusion and should you be able to create this effect, you can be sure that you are a somnambulistic subject. Here are suggestions you can use:

"As I count to three, I shall gradually feel the cool ocean breeze coming over the waves. It will be a very pleasant feeling. One... I am beginning to feel the cool ocean breeze, especially on my face and hands. Two... The breeze is becoming stronger and stronger. Three... I can definitely feel the cool ocean breeze. As I continue to count to five, I shall smell the pleasant, healthy aroma of the salt water. Four... I am beginning to smell the salt water. Five... I can definitely smell the salt water."

Now you give yourself appropriate suggestions that the feeling (illusion) will vanish as you awaken or at a specific count. It can be as simple as this: "As I count to three, I shall open my eyes and awaken feeling very refreshed. The feeling of the cool ocean breeze and smell of the salt air will have vanished completely." At this point you count to three and open your eyes.

Test No. 10 is the "handclasp" test. This is used frequently to test the depth of hypnosis. You fold your hands with your fingers tightly interlocked and place your palms together. You then give yourself a hypnotic suggestion that at the count of three, it will be impossible for you to unlock your hands. After you try and are unable to unlock your hands, you continue counting to five, suggesting that you will be able to do so when you reach the count of five. Incidentally, you should remove any ring you may be wearing before trying this test. Here are the suggestions you can follow:

"As I complete the count of three, I shall try to unlock

my hands but will be unable to do so until I count to five. One...My hands are locked tightly together. Two...My fingers are locked tighter and tighter. Three...It is impossible for me to unlock my hands until I count to five. Four...As I reach the count of five, I shall be able to unlock my hands very easily. Five...I can now unlock my hands very easily."

Test No. 11 is the "arm" test. Here is another test used frequently to test the receptiveness to hypnosis. Make a tight fist and extend your arm in front of you as far as possible. Visualize your arm as one solid mass, as stiff and rigid as a bar of steel. After your arm is extended, give yourself a hypnotic suggestion that you will be unable to bend your arm when you complete the count of three. As you continue to count to five, you will be able to bend your arm very easily. Here is a form of suggestion you can use:

"As I reach the count of three, I shall try to bend my arm, but it will be impossible to do so until I count to five. No matter how hard I try, it will be absolutely impossible. One...My arm is stiff and rigid as a bar of steel. Two...I can feel the rigidity in my arm. Three...It is impossible for me to bend my arm until I count to five. Four...I can feel the stiffness slowly leaving. Five...I can now bend my arm easily and it feels normal in every respect."

Test No. 12 is the "eye" test. This is probably the most widely used test in hypnosis. Many subjects equate the inability to open the eyes with hypnosis. Many assume that if they can open their eyes, they have not been hypnotized. I must emphatically point out that this is not true. The subject can fail the eye test and yet have been under hypnosis. In the deep, somnambulistic state, the subject can open his eyes without affecting the depth of the hypnotic state. In fact, this is done many times in getting the subject to do automatic writing, crystal gazing, mirror gazing, hypnodrama and revivification. In carrying out posthypnotic suggestions in any state, the subject is frequently told that he will open his eyes and carry out the suggestion.

I have found that there is more anxiety connected with the eye test than with any other test. I feel that it is a normal reaction and one that must be anticipated by the hypnotist as well as the subject. Occasionally, while hypnotizing a new subject, he will open his eyes. This can happen when the subject feels he is losing consciousness. His ability to open his eyes proves to him that he is in control. One of the main fears that the subject has is his belief that he will lose voluntary control of himself. The fact that he can open his eyes lessens his anxiety.

If there seems to be too much threat to the individual, I use a method that you can follow. Instead of suggesting that the subject will be unable to open his eyes at a specific count, I suggest that he will be so relaxed that it will be too much effort to open his eyes until a further count is given. Actually, what could take less effort? Here are suggestions you can use:

"As I count to three, I shall try to open my eyes, but I shall be unable to do so because I feel so relaxed. It will just take too much effort to open my eyes until I reach the count of five or tell myself to awaken. One...My eyes are closed, and I am in a very deep state of hypnosis. Two... My eyelids are stuck tightly together. Three...It is now impossible for me to open my eyes. I shall be able to open them though at the count of five. Four...I shall be able to open my eyes very easily at the count of five. Five...I can now open my eyes and wake up feeling alert and fully refreshed."

In accomplishing the eye test, you try to create a vivid picture of yourself being completely and fully relaxed. If you really exerted a great deal of effort, you could open your eyes, but because of the pleasantness of the completely relaxed state, you prefer not to do so. It can be likened to your enduring the cold winter air when you are half asleep in bed instead of getting up to close the window which has been left open too much. You can, of course, get up and close the window, but it becomes a matter of expending too much energy. Instead, you choose to endure the discomfort or suggest that your spouse close the window.

For the following three tests, you give yourself the suggestions as outlined in the previous tests. It should be pointed out again that at the conclusion of the test, you give yourself a suggestion that you will feel normal in every respect.

Test No. 13 is the "music" test. This test involves creating an auditory hallucination. Give yourself the suggestion that at a specific count you will hear your favorite song. It will last for one minute and then fade out.

Test No. 14 is the "dream" test. It is incorporated in a great deal of hypnotherapy. The subject is told that as the hypnotist counts to three, the subject will have a dream lasting for several minutes which he will remember. This dream, furthermore, will call his attention to an important incident that he has long forgotten, yet which will be relevant to his problem. In self-hypnosis, you suggest to yourself that at a specific count you will have a very pleasant dream lasting for several minutes, at the end of which time you will awaken feeling refreshed. For those readers further interested in producing dreams, I can highly recommend a very fascinating book called *The Experimental Production of Dreams During Hypnosis* by Professor David Ballin Klein.

Test No. 15 is the "anesthesia" test. This is conducted by telling yourself that you will not feel the pain associated with the act of pinching yourself. You suggest that you will feel the pressure of your fingers but will not feel the pain involved. *I urge the reader not to stick pins in himself to test the anesthesia. This can be dangerous, lead to infection and cause other harmful results.* You should also not dig your nails into your skin to make sure that you don't feel pain.

Chapter 10

A New Approach to Self-Hypnosis
When All Else Fails

Let us assume that you have tried diligently to learn self-hypnosis for a month or more but have failed. You have worked faithfully following the instructions outlined in this book and other books on self-hypnosis, but somehow the state of hypnosis eludes you. Should you give up in despair, or is there still hope for you? Let me assure you that you can still become an excellent subject. Let us examine several areas of this problem and a new approach that will help you achieve your ends.

You must, first of all, ask yourself if you are feeling better and whether you have made strides in the direction you desire while giving yourself suggestions in whatever stage of hypnosis you have achieved. If your evaluation is affirmative to any degree, you can expect even greater results. "But," you may say, "how can I expect greater results when I haven't achieved self-hypnosis?" My answer is you may be achieving self-hypnosis and not know it! The change to the self-hypnotic state from the waking state can be imperceptible. Many times, prior to testing subjects under hypnosis, I ask them if they think they are in the hypnotic state. The answer is invariably no. When asking the subjects for a cogent reason for this answer, they usually exclaim that they are aware of what is going on and do not feel any different than they did before I started working with them. They are amazed to find that various tests work so perfectly.

Some subjects do not respond to hypnotic tests no matter how long you work with them. For these persons, I usually de-emphasize the need for passing the tests and concentrate on the therapeutic results which are desired. This approach lessens anxiety and usually results in a deepening of the hypnotic state. It is my feeling that many subjects resist any tests as the implication is that once the tests work, the subject is under complete control of the hypnotist. The subject may fear this supposed subjection on one hand and yet want it on the other hand. These forces can work unconsciously, and thus the attainment of hypnosis becomes a very intricate, perplexing and trying procedure. Even though this may be so, I can assure you that the problem and attainment of hypnosis can be re-solved. It is only a matter of motivation on the part of the subject. This is the main ingredient necessary for success-ful hypnosis.

Let me now explain a technique which has worked admirably for many who have been frustrated because of their inability to achieve self-hypnosis. It involves *pretend-ing you are hypnotized* and going through the motions of the various tests *as though you were a perfect subject.* You will recall that one theory of hypnosis is that the sub-ject behaves in a manner that he believes is in keeping with hypnotic behavior. This role playing is the basis for our unique approach. As the subject continues this procedure, he takes on the conditioned response mechanism necessary for self-hypnosis. Let us look at the following examples of role playing.

During the war, many soldiers who wanted to leave the army would pretend something was wrong with them. They would convince the authorities of the authenticity of their "illness," and since nothing seemed to make them better, they eventually were separated from the service because of the incapacitating disorder. But what happened to many of these malingerers after they were released from the service? I'm sure you know the rest of the story. The constant malingering was transformed by this role playing into a conditioned response pattern, eventually bringing about the very undesirable condition responsible for their leaving the service. I saw some of these individuals and more than once they told me that they had unwittingly hypnotized themselves into having the ailment. They wanted me to dehypnotize them. They actually turned out to be very easy subjects as they had become highly suggestible. Unfortunately, their super-ego structure was weak, they had difficulty in identifying strongly with anyone, and the relationship in hypnosis was superficial and without depth.

I am going to relate another example which I hope will help you understand the role-playing technique for self-hypnosis. I have had the following experience many times in giving hypnotic demonstrations before various organizations. For some reason, even though I carefully ask that only those who desire to be hypnotized volunteer as subjects for the hypnotic demonstrations, an individual who has no intention of cooperating comes up on the stage to poke fun at the hypnotist. In giving public demonstrations, I usually work with about ten subjects and simultaneously give them the same suggestions and posthypnotic suggestions. Once the subjects are hypnotized, I work with them with their eyes open. Using this technique, with each subject carrying out a posthypnotic suggestion, intensifies the responses of other subjects. There is also competitiveness to become the best subject.

In the meantime, the individual who is really not under hypnosis has let the audience know about it by winking or making a grimace when I was not looking at him. Observing laughter and other audience reactions which are not in keeping with what is happening at the precise moment during my lecture is my cue that I have an egocentric person on stage. You might ask, "Can't you tell when someone is faking?" It is extremely difficult many times to do so. Once you are aware of it, however, you give certain tests to the group. The exhibitionist doesn't know how to respond each time and you soon pick him out.

Even when I know specifically who it is, I do not dismiss him. Interestingly, it is invariably a man. I continue with the lecture-demonstration; but I let the audience know that I am aware of the situation. This is the interesting part of this example. The bumptious subject, by giving himself autosuggestions to comply with various posthypnotic suggestions, is actually engaging in our technique of role playing. The inevitable happens. He finds himself hypnotized despite his obvious intention not to be affected in any way. Any hypnotist can recount similar incidents.

What can you learn by the example just presented? What if you purposely set about doing the same thing in your attempt to achieve self-hypnosis? The obvious answer is that the technique has a good chance of working, and as a result you will achieve self-hypnosis. This method has worked with many recalcitrant subjects. To follow this plan, go back to chapter six, "How To Attain Self-Hypnosis," and use the role-playing technique. You'll be pleasantly surprised at how this approach will act as a catalyst. Remember, once you obtain the eye closure, give yourself whatever therapeutic suggestion you desire plus the posthypnotic suggestion that the next time you will fall into a deeper and sounder state of hypnosis at the count of three or any other cue you desire.

I know you may protest using the role-playing technique with the question, "If I'm not under hypnosis, why give myself therapeutic posthypnotic suggestions to condition myself to go under hypnosis at a specific count?" You may further protest that you are only fooling yourself. My answer is, "What if you are?" What is lost by doing it? You have everything to gain and nothing to lose. Are you not really interested in the end result and not the means? The attainment of the self-hypnotic state is not in itself the end result; it is a means to help you achieve your goal.

Don't many people carry or wear good-luck charms of a religious or nonreligious nature? Don't we accept these items in our society? The four-leaf clover and rabbit's foot as symbols of good luck have been part of our culture for a long time. We are all sophisticated enough to know that they do not have an intrinsic value, but don't they do something for our mental attitude? This same pattern is precisely what you are to follow in using the role-playing technique. If you believe, expect and imagine that you will be successful in this approach to self-hypnosis, I can assure you that you will.

May I urge you not to reject this novel and unorthodox approach. Many have had excellent results when other methods, even those of a professional hypnotist, have failed. Some of you may recognize this approach as another means of applying the visual-imagery technique. Whatever you choose to call it, I reiterate you can expect good results. It is only necessary that you follow the instructions and adopt the right attitude. By the right attitude, I mean that you should adopt the conviction that you are going to achieve self-hypnosis even though you might have experienced difficulty up to now. Hypnosis is a conviction phenomenon.

It is possible you may say you are not suggestible. Actually, your lack of response proves your suggestibility. You have been influenced by negative suggestions. Everyone is suggestible to some degree. You have become extremely suggestible to conscious or unconscious stimuli which are definitely affecting your ability to respond. You need only use this latent suggestibility and make it work for you. What would you say about the suggestibility of a person who doesn't want to talk about hypnosis? This person has never read a book on hypnosis and absolutely doesn't want you or anyone else to hypnotize him. Would you believe this person is a potentially good hypnotic subject? I can tell you by practical experience that once this person allows himself to be hypnotized, he turns out to be a perfect subject. Responding to either end of the suggestibility scale is indicative of success with hypnosis. It becomes a matter of manipulating this suggestibility skillfully in order to achieve results.

Let me give you another example which may help. Which one of the two lines drawn on this page is longer? Line AB or line CD?

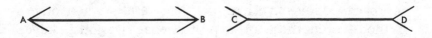

What is your answer? Did you think both were the same? Take a ruler and actually measure them. You'll find line AB longer than CD. "But," you reply, "every other time both lines were the same." This is a familiar optical illusion which is used many times in basic courses in psychology. It is known as the Muller-Lyer illusion. My contention is that if you said, "Both are the same size," you are potentially a good subject. You respond perfectly to previous conditioning; thus, you are responding as anticipated. If, on the other hand, you picked line AB, you are normally suggestible. If you honestly picked line CD, you are extremely cautious and respond best to "reverse psychology." Once again you are highly suggestible, but toward one extreme.

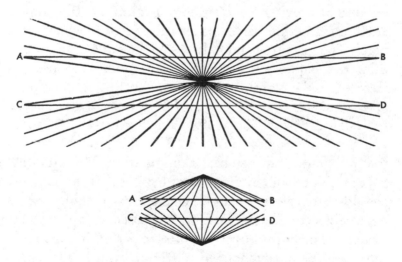

Here's another interesting experiment. Would you say that lines AB and CD were perfectly straight? I'll let you figure out what your response means to this test by yourself. You can take a ruler to determine if the lines are straight.

We all respond unconsciously to stimuli of some sort. Word association tests are based on this principle. Aren't your reactions automatic to the following terms: democratic party, republican party, communist party, mother, father, movie star? If I mention the name of a famous person, city or country, the same immediate unconscious reaction takes place. Let's try it. Theodore Roósevelt, Harry Truman, Dwight D. Eisenhower, John F. Kennedy, Albert Einstein, Albert Schweitzer, Eleanor Roosevelt, Boston, New York City, Hollywood, Miami Beach, United States, England, France, Italy, Israel, Africa, Russia, China, India and South America. The response and image keep changing, don't they?

I am trying to point out that this reaction is automatic because of previous conditioning. I could mention almost anything and the same automatic reaction would take place. The reaction would always be the same unless something had happened to change or alter your response. Let us mention the word hypnosis. Some sort of reaction must take place. This can either be positive, negative, or neutral for our purposes. You really don't have to think about your response as it is automatic. The point to remember is that a definite response has taken place which will either help or hinder your attainment of hypnosis. If the response should be negative, it can be changed by gaining knowledge and actual experience in hypnosis. It is natural to have a bit of uneasiness when first experiencing or thinking about being hypnotized. After all, you haven't been exposed to hypnosis in a therapeutic setting and couldn't have formed a favorable reaction. Your response is probably derived from a fictionization of hypnosis. The initial task of the hypnotist is to create, by educating the prospective subject, a favorable attitude so that the subject allows himself to be hypnotized.

What does this mean specifically to you if you are having difficulty learning self-hypnosis? It means that through repeated exposures, you will finally respond. You will realize there is no need for anxiety in regard to your response. This inner feeling will, in turn, have a cumulative, favorable effect upon your unconscious which will result in your finally responding to hypnosis.

Suppose you still maintain and insist that you are not suggestible and wonder if you will ever respond to hypnosis. Furthermore, the assurance I have given you up to this point doesn't seem to convince you. If you have tried diligently to achieve self-hypnosis, you cannot be blamed, but let's try an experiment to test your suggestibility. It is well to ponder my statement that if you do not respond, it is a sign of being suggestible, but in a negative sense. Lack of response is a manifestation of this negative suggestibility. My contention is that you are definitely suggestible. Let us see what happens to you in trying the following classical experiment. It is called the Chevreul's Pendulum test.

Draw a circle with about a six-inch diameter and mark it as shown in the illustration.

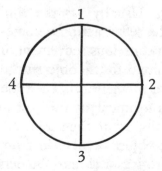

Next, take a ring and attach a string to it. If you have a locket, it will do as well. The hypnotist uses a crystal ball and chain for this experiment. Hold the end of the string or chain and keep the ring or whatever object you are using about three inches above the center of the circle.

Now, concentrate and fix your gaze on the ring, crystal ball, or locket. Mentally suggest to yourself that the object will begin to revolve in a circular manner following the numbers 1, 2, 3, and 4. Picture in your mind's eye that this circular motion is becoming wider and wider. Work at this image for several minutes. Did the object begin turning to the right following the numbers? Did the circle become larger and larger? If it did, you are absolutely suggestible, are influenced by your own suggestions and, therefore, if you follow instructions, can learn self-hypnosis. You can be trained to acquire this skill.

If the experience did not work, try it again. Concentrate harder and try to visualize more intently the object revolving in a circular manner. You are not to rotate the object consciously or help it in any way. The action must stem from your subconscious. The thought of the crystal ball or ring revolving in a clockwise or counterclockwise direction invariably causes an involuntary muscular reflex action to take place. This phenomenon is known as an ideomotor action. Usually, as the subject concentrates more intensely, the reflex action becomes more profound, causing greater unconscious movement of the hand which, in turn, is transmitted to the object in the form of larger circles and greater momentum. The time required for the successful accomplishment of this test depends upon the degree of suggestibility of the subject. An interesting action is to see the object revolve in an opposite direction than suggested. It gives a clue to the personality structure of the individual.

The Ouija board works on the same principle as the

Chevreul's Pendulum test. Many times the aspirant will remark, "I swear I didn't make it move!" Mentalists find hidden objects in an audience using basically the same approach, combined with clever techniques of distraction. The term given for this is "muscle reading."

This is the point in question. If the crystal ball, ring or locket moves without conscious direction, you have successfully influenced your subconscious mind. Self-hypnosis involves the same procedure. The goal is to consciously cause a subconscious reaction. If the experiment does not work with your eyes open, try it with your eyes closed for about five minutes. You will be pleasantly surprised with the results. Should you want to prove to yourself that you are suggestible with your eyes open, practice the technique every day for a week or two. The idea of the practice sessions is to reinforce and increase the response of the unconscious movement until you develop proficiency. It follows the laws of the conditioned reflex theory expounded by Dr. Ivan P. Pavlov (1849-1936), the famous Russian psychologist. If, after several weeks, you should still not be successful, use the role-playing technique. Consciously make the object revolve. After a while, it will move automatically whenever you attempt the experiment.

When this happens you will have proof of your suggestibility. It is highly improbable that you will not be successful. It would be a rare occurrence. By the same systematic efforts, I can assure you that you can achieve self-hypnosis. If you are still not affected favorably, you might consider one of the psychological means of inducing hypnosis. The next chapter will discuss this topic.

I would recommend Pavlov's book called *Conditioned Reflexes*. Pavlov's book will further explain and clarify the concept of the conditioned response mechanism. It covers necessary conditions for the development of conditioned responses, their formation by means of conditioned and direct stimuli, plus a tremendous amount of material which will help you in your understanding of the significance of the role-playing technique in relationship to learning self-hypnosis.

Chapter 11

Psychological Aids and Their Function

Psychological or mechanical aids are used to help put the subject in a state of hypnosis. The use of the aids helps increase the suggestibility of the subject toward hypnosis. The two most widely used hypnotic aids are the crystal ball and chain and the 12-inch hypnodisc. One reason is that these two items have no other use or function outside of the area of hypnosis. Therefore, when the hypnotist proceeds to use one of these hypnotic devices, it must follow that a certain mental set, readiness, or receptivity must follow as a result of its introduction into the hypnotic setting. If the subject is uneasy about the hypnotic setting or his response, the introduction of the hypnotic aid can mobilize the subject's defenses which may be on a conscious or unconscious level. Generally, the mental set which follows helps augment whatever hypnotic suggestions are given. Certainly the same mental set would not follow if the hypnotist used a paper clip as a means of helping with the induction of hypnosis. It would only start the subject wondering about the relationship of the paper clip to hypnosis. It obviously isn't in keeping with what the subject expects.

It is important to utilize the subject's expectation as to what he believes takes place in the setting as long as this expectation does not hinder the induction of hypnosis. The mere act of turning down the lights or drawing the curtains before the hypnotist begins to work with the subject is a non-verbal suggestion which can be considered as a psychological aid. The subject knows that the hypnotist is ready to begin at this point. Actually, it isn't necessary to darken the room at any time to induce hypnosis. Doesn't the stage hypnotist work with glaring lights? The room is darkened (and I might add that I use this procedure myself) mainly for the psychological effect. If I feel that this procedure might cause anxiety, I proceed with the room undarkened.

In discussing psychological aids, it is agreed that we are primarily interested in seeing the subject feel better or achieve whatever goals he seeks through the intelligent application of self-hypnosis. If a hypnotic aid will help the subject achieve hypnosis, we can concur it is justified. It is not to be considered a subterfuge. If the physician administers a placebo to a patient with the remark, "Here is a new medication that can help your condition" and if this technique does help alleviate the patient's condition, it is considered good medicine.

You know beforehand that in using the 12-inch hypnodisc, the subject's eyes must begin to water, his eyelids must get heavy, and eventually he must close them. Even before you begin to use the hypnodisc, you suggest that these conditions will take place. During the induction of hypnosis, as these reactions are noted by the subject, a favorable, psychological attitude automatically develops which, in turn, helps further suggestions. If the subject reacts favorably to suggestions A, B, and C, it follows that he is more prone to accept suggestions D, E, and F which are therapeutic in nature. The subject can relate better to the latter suggestions when he has seen proof of his initial suggestibility. This approach works better than beginning immediately with the latter suggestions. The build-up of suggestions convinces the subject he is in a heightened state of suggestibility and can benefit from the therapeutic suggestions of the hypnotist or his own. Perhaps this needed assurance is so helpful because it eliminates the anxiety of the subject concerning his suggestibility. He seeks and needs the satisfaction of knowing he has attained the prerequisites necessary before any therapeutic program can benefit him. The subject's prerequisites need not be actually related to the hypnotic process, per se, but merely match his preconceived ideas about what is necessary. Let me give you an example.

Many subjects feel that they must experience amnesia before they can benefit from hypnotic suggestions. This premise is inaccurate since favorable and lasting results can be achieved in any degree of hypnosis, depending, of course, on the nature of the problem. Let me relate several interesting occurrences that take place every so often in my own practice as a professional hypnotist. A subject who is responding well to hypnosis, but not to the point of amnesia, insists that he will not benefit until he is "knocked out" and doesn't remember what happened. Trying to convince him otherwise proves fatal. He just refuses to accept whatever explanation you give him. My own method is not to insist that the subject is wrong, but somehow to use his misconception in a constructive manner. After getting him into a cataleptic state, I suggest that I am going to stop talking for five minutes, during which time he is to mentally repeat "sleep" as he slowly and deeply inhales and "deep sleep" as he slowly exhales. At the end of this time, he'll be in a very deep hypnotic state. Instead of remaining quiet for five minutes, I take ten minutes. I then begin to whisper suggestions to the subject to determine if he is still under hypnosis or asleep. If he is asleep, I let him remain asleep for a still longer period of time, after which interval I awaken him. I ask him if he remembers what I said to him during the time he was deeply hypnotized. If he says, "No," I remark, "Very good." I further point out to him that he has now experienced amnesia and will now make rapid strides. The subject, on the other hand, is pleased to see that I now agree with him, and, in fact, the interesting result is that he does make excellent progress because his preconceived requirements have been met. It should be pointed out that I keep working with the subject until such time that he falls asleep. The transition from hypnosis to sleep is normal. It is easy for the subject to fall asleep because he is so relaxed.

Let me tell you of a similar experience. Before telling you of this psychological technique, it is only fair to point out that the professional hypnotist varies his approach from subject to subject, not only to suit the needs of the subject but to break the monotony of using only a few successful procedures. His experimentation helps develop not only new procedures, but new concepts relative to the general nature of hypnosis and its many ramifications. I was interested to see what would happen to a subject if he thought he was deeply hypnotized without ever giving him verbal suggestions or reassurance that he would feel better or overcome his problem. Of course, if the technique did not work quickly, I would drop the procedure for a more orthodox approach. Instead of trying to really hypnotize the subject, my aim is to get him to sleep. Once he is asleep, I let him remain so for about 30 minutes. Without having ever given him a therapeutic suggestion, I awaken him and inquire if he remembered what happened. If the answer is, "No," I tell him I'll "hypnotize" him again next week and this concludes the visit. When he returns next week, I ask him, "How did you feel during the week?" The answer is generally, "Much better." I keep repeating this procedure until such time that the individual has attained the goals that he seeks.

I know that the reader may be surprised that I would divulge such an unconventional procedure. The principle is the same as the physician using a placebo. I do so to illustrate the point that I made earlier in this chapter that so long as certain of the subject's requirements are met, whether valid or invalid, the subject's suggestibility is greatly enhanced. Naturally, the unsuspecting subject equated the period of not remembering, which was, as we know, true sleep, with the somnambulistic state. Actually, he was helped by self-hypnosis because he felt he would now make progress because he proved to be such an excellent subject. It is true, he was not using self-hypnosis as has been outlined in this book, but he had now achieved a heightened state of suggestibility (hypnosis) and was using this state to further his own ends.

The attainment of self-hypnosis can be an intricate and elusive procedure as I have already pointed out. The purpose of the entire book is to instruct, point out and give you the necessary understanding and knowledge required to achieve this end. Without this understanding, this can become a very frustrating effort. It is hoped that by under-standing and being aware of some of the ramifications of hypnosis, you will be able to achieve your goal in the quickest possible time. It should also be pointed out that no two subjects react in the same way and that different methods and requirements are necessary to suit the indi-vidual. It is a mistake to try to make the subject adhere to a rigid methodology. The greater flexibility of the hyp-notic procedures, the greater the chance for success. Let me, at this time, further discuss some of the hypnotic aids that are used in the induction of hypnosis.

We have already discussed the use of the hypnodisc and crystal ball and chain. The same principles are involved in any other object which is used as a means of fixation or of tiring the eyes. Hypnotic phonograph records and hyp-notic tape recordings represent new devices that have been instrumental in conditioning subjects for self-hypnosis. The subject plays the record or tape on his phonograph or tape recorder and is conditioned over a period of time to respond to hypnosis at a given signal or phrase. He, in turn, can change this key phrase to one of his own choos-ing. Should you own or have access to a tape recorder, I would suggest recording an induction of hypnosis and playing it back to yourself in this manner as though you were hypnotizing someone else.

I have produced three different hypnotic records and a 30-minute hypnotic tape containing the three records which are sold commercially. One record, called the Musical Hypnotic Record, has a very pleasant, relaxing musical background as the voice of the hypnotist induces hypnosis. The second record, called the Metronome Hyp-notic Record, incorporates the monotonous and lulling beat of an electric metronome in the background. The subject is instructed to mentally repeat "sleep" as he slowly inhales and "deep sleep" as he slowly exhales in rhythm with the beat of the metronome. While the subject is concentrating on this activity, the voice of the hypnotist induces hypnosis. The third record, called Self-Hypnosis Record No. 3, contains only the voice of the hypnotist inducing hypnosis. It features a unique approach and technique.

I have had a great deal of correspondence with those who have used these phonograph records and the hypnotic tape for conditioning themselves for self-hypnosis. The results are quite interesting and run the range of immediate results to no results. One person wrote that one of the records hypnotized him at the first playing and conditioned him for self-hypnosis, whereas he had failed to respond to hypnosis after many visits to one of the country's foremost authorities. I have had similar experiences after having failed to hypnotize a subject despite many attempts. I can only speculate that the subjects in these cases unconsciously resist the hypnotist because they feel a personal threat. Since the record is impersonal, they are better able to relax and subsequently be hypnotized. Interestingly, this occurred when the subject was convinced that he was a very difficult subject. It would seem that only then was the conditioned response pattern finally established. The basic function of the hypnotic records and hypnotic tape is to establish a conditioned response pattern to a given stimulus. In time, most subjects are conditioned by the intelligent and systematic use of these recordings.

Let me describe another varied approach to achieving self-hypnosis. One of the chief assets of a good hypnotist is to be flexible in his approach in hypnotizing his subjects. As I have already pointed out, it is necessary many times to adopt a technique that is suitable to the subject and not to make the subject adapt himself to the method of induction.

We know that with somnambulistic subjects any procedure will put the subject under hypnosis immediately. The hypnotist gains complete control of his subject as the subject is able to put himself in the proper psychological frame of mind for hypnosis. Unfortunately, most subjects do not respond at the first session or sessions because of conscious or subconscious fears that must be gradually eliminated. Once you get the subject to relax, or "let go," he will naturally succumb to hypnosis. This is the problem that confronts all hypnotists.

Merely suggesting to the subject to relax is not sufficient, as a rule, to bring about this desired mental state. The subject, at this point, cannot easily turn on or off his mental and physical feelings. Even if we have the subject lie down, this does not assure the hypnotic state as the subject can still be tense. Our main problem is to get the subject relaxed. Our situation is similar to the physician telling his patient to go home and forget about a certain problem. I'm sure you'll agree that the advice is virtually impossible to follow.

One of the major stumbling blocks in hypnotizing a subject or in self-hypnosis lies in the fact that although we use terms such as "relax," "let yourself go," and others, the subject cannot readily put the meaning of these words into effect. It is difficult for most people to let go when we live in a society that beckons us to "look sharp," "be sharp," "be alert," "be on the ball" and "make every minute count." Emphasis on productivity does not lend to a society of relaxed individuals.

Psychological Aids and Their Function

In my long experience as a professional hypnotist, I have tried many novel innovations for inducing hypnosis and teaching individuals self-hypnosis. Some have met with a great deal of success and others have failed. It is, furthermore, difficult to determine the causal factors for success or failure. We can only theorize.

I have used the following unorthodox technique for about a period of 15 years. Exceptionally good results have been attained with it, although it must be admitted that it is not infallible. It is suggested to you as another good technique. In order to help the subject relax, I have been using a phonograph record or tape that I recorded containing the continuous sound of various degrees of rain. One side has a half hour of very soft, light rainfall such as you have experienced in listening to rain falling on grass, canvas or a tent top. The other side or track contains a half hour of rain effects such as one would hear in a heavy downfall with loud splatterings of water on the pavement. The record and tape were originally designed to help insomnia sufferers and later incorporated into the hypnotic procedure.

The subject is instructed to close his eyes and listen to the sound of the rain while picturing himself relaxing near a warm, glowing fireplace. As you can note, the subject again incorporates the visual-imagery technique. The relaxing effect thus produced over a period of time enhances his chances of success in attaining a deep, hypnotic state.

There are many other interesting and unique devices and aids you can use for inducing hypnosis.

Chapter 12

The Nature of Hypnosis

Although the nature and phenomena of hypnosis are still incompletely understood, there are a multitude of theories which attempt to explain its mechanism and results. The most that can be done at this time is to explore various views which are held by leading authorities at present. It can be said, however, that a majority of authorities agree that hypnosis ensues as a result of natural laws which have been incorporated in the human organism since the beginning of man as he is today.

The older theories show almost as much disparity as today, but for the purposes of history it is probably necessary to enumerate only the "animal magnetism" of Frederick Anton Mesmer, and a mention of the "hysteria syndrome" of Jean Martin Charcot. Both names loom large in the history of hypnosis. Mesmer, an 18th century physician, believed that hypnosis occurred as a result of "vital fluids" drawn from a magnet or lodestone and which drew their unique qualities from the sun, moon and stars. Charcot, as well as Pierre Janet and others, was convinced that hypnosis was a form of hysteria and that only hysterics could be hypnotized. The former (Mesmer) thought further that metal became imbued by the solar qualities, and his system is also known as metalogy by which he meant the proper application of metals. Naturally, these theories have been largely abandoned today, although there are still a few who think that hypnosis is a form of hysteria.

Some pioneers, notably Dr. William S. Kroger, a psychiatrically-oriented obstetrician and gynecologist who limits his practice to hypnotherapy, believe hypnosis is a conviction phenomenon which produces results that parallel the phenomena produced at Lourdes and other religious healing shrines. His formula is that faith, hope, belief and expectation, all catalyzed by the imagination, lead inevitably to hypnosis. He, like Emile Coué before him, is convinced that you cannot "will" yourself to be hypnotized, and that whenever the will and the imagination come into conflict, the imagination wins out. This fits in perfectly, of course, with the author's already discussed visual-imagery technique which requires a high degree of imagination. Dr. Kroger, like a few others, has proved to his own satisfaction that all hypnotic phenomena can be produced at a non-hypnotic level.

A large number of hypnotists, including the author, has come to believe that hypnosis is a semantic problem in which words are the building blocks to success. Not just any words, but words which "ring a bell" or tap the experiential background of the subject. This is why "sleep" continues to be in the lexicon of the hypnotist even though hypnosis is the antithesis of sleep. The word is used because hypnosis superficially resembles sleep inasmuch as the eyes usually are closed, the body in a posture of complete relaxation. Actually, the mind is hyperacute. Pavlov, however, believed that there was an analogy between sleep and hypnosis in that each involved cerebral inhibition. Words, of course, would be of little use without the added effect of his conditioned reflexology.

Probably the most widely held theory is that hypnosis is a transference phenomenon in which the prestige of the hypnotist and his relationship to the subject plays an important role. This theory is bolstered by the fact that all schools of psychotherapy yield approximately the same results even though the methods differ. This would logically indicate that the relationship between the therapist and the subject was the determining factor. The only trouble with this theory is that it does not explain self-hypnosis. On the other hand, we know that a strong interpersonal relationship is necessary for hypnosis.

In the opening chapter of the book, I explained that hypnosis was a state of heightened suggestion in which the subject adopted an uncritical attitude, allowing him to accept suggestions and to take appropriate action. This is excellent as far as it goes, but it does not explain how suggestion works. This is the crux of the hypnotic dilemma and the answer is far from solved. Hypnotists are much like those who use electricity every day of their lives, but have no idea of the nature of electricity. It is enough for them to know it has been harnessed for their use.

If there is one thing virtually certain about hypnosis it is that some parts of the brain are inhibited and other parts expanded by the process. Pin-point concentration is given as the reason for this selective procedure which narrows the horizon of the subject to what the hypnotist (or he, himself) is saying, screening out all other stimuli.

But why is this high order of concentration so easy under hypnosis when Asians, notably the Chinese, have been trying for centuries to concentrate on one subject for as long as four or five seconds. We do not know the mechanics of this metamorphosis of an ordinary brain into an organ of concentrated power. According to Janet, this is accomplished through the formation of a group of unconscious memories and activities which takes over the usual stream-of-consciousness type of thinking. It is implied that the process may be atavistic.

One of the newer theories—one held by Dr. Lewis R. Wolberg, a psychoanalyst—is that hypnosis is a psychosomatic process in that it is both physiological and psychological in character. Physiologically, Wolberg believes that hypnosis represents an inhibition of the higher cortical centers, and a limitation of sensory channels such as takes place in sleep. He also believes that the psychological process operates through transference. Others agree that it is a transference process, but that it is more of an extension of the subject's own psychic processes which is enlarged to include the voice of the hypnotist or his own thoughts or voice. Incidentally, an excellent book along these theoretical lines is *Hypnotism—An Objective Study in Suggestibility* by André M. Weitzenhoffer, Ph.D.

The newest theory in the field is of particular interest to those reading this book inasmuch as it postulates that all hypnosis is self-hypnosis, that the patient always hypnotizes himself and that it is a wise hypnotist who knows who is hypnotizing whom. This is a logical conclusion and it disperses any ideas that hypnotic patients become dependent on their therapists. Actually, hypnotists today always teach their subjects self-hypnosis so that any chance of dependency is obviated.

Milton V. Kline, professor of psychology at Long Island University, postulates that hypnosis is primarily retrogressive. He has written that the organism functions differently on various levels of behavior (regression), and that the behavior breaks down into component parts. The theory that regression can spotlight personality disorders found in more infantile states is also widely held. He also is a proponent of the idea that hypnosis is an abnormal manifestation of a normal process, an opinion he shares with many.

Dr. Kline thinks that retrogression and regression alter perceptions and feelings, and, in the case of the latter, causes us to go backward in time to the point where re-education may be employed. This is a legitimate use of regression although it is not used so much these days to uncover past traumatic incidents. Actually, regression, by duplicating the exact earlier age, manner of speech and thought, etc., makes us once more as little children, a condition to be desired for certain forms of therapy.

An atavistic theory, held to some extent by Dr. Jerome M. Schneck, clinical associate professor of psychiatry, State University of New York College of Medicine, is that hypnosis should be equated with states of immobilization on the basis of his observation that some subjects equate hypnosis with "death." He suggests this is comparable to the "death-feint" of animals to avoid danger. Others, primarily Europeans, have pointed out the analogy between the hypnotic state of animals and man.

Another widely-held theory is that hypnosis is a state of dissociation, meaning that it constitutes a group of unconscious memories and activities which may be dredged up to replace the stream of consciousness. Automaticism, of course, is inherently part of this view, and is presumed to negate volition. Activity of the cerebrum, which controls the conscious and voluntary system, is rendered non-operational.

My own thoughts on the matter are that hypnosis results from, first of all, a good transference; secondly, from a conditioned reflex; thirdly, from the person acting as a hypnotized person (role playing), and, fourthly, from a suspension of the critical faculties. Along the last-named line, I believe that hypnotic suggestions have an autonomy of their own which supersede all else in the hypnotic situation. There are many more theories I believe are partially correct, but the ones named will do for the purposes of this volume. Incidentally, all the hypnosis theories presented are equally applicable to self-hypnosis except where, as in transference, it is obvious a therapist is needed.

In conclusion, the author would like to take issue with those who believe that it is the monotonous intonations of the therapist that cause the subject to lapse from the deeply relaxed state into true sleep. I have observed many times, by comparing verbalization with silence, that the former gives the subject's mind a focal point of attention which prevents him from entering a sleep state where hypnotherapy is impossible. Like the man who cannot sleep because of an active mind, sleep and myriad thoughts and suggestions are incompatible, and I believe, once a hypnotic state has been attained, that the subject is kept awake (unless definite sleep suggestions are given) by the therapist's series of suggestions. We have discussed the effect of the experiential background at length, and surely nothing connotates sleep more than closing one's eyes—test No. 1. And so, in my view, you are doing two things when you talk to the subject; you are giving him helpful suggestions, but you are also keeping him awake and hyperacute so that these suggestions will sink in.

Practical Applications of Self-Hypnosis

With hypnosis on the march, there is practically no limit to its uses in the field of medicine, and new applications are being discovered every day. It should not be necessary to add, however, that some of these uses should remain as they are—in the hands of professionals with years of experience in the area. One of the themes of this book has been that laymen should use hypnosis discriminately and intelligently. No responsible therapist would ever recommend masking or removing a symptom which was indicative of organic disease. For that reason, the practical uses of self-hypnosis will be limited to measures that can be taken safely by the layman. The only possible exception to this will be instructions on how to curb obesity, but even here it is suggested that a physician be consulted before embarking on a weight-reducing program.

The foremost use of hypnosis has been for relaxation, and it becomes more and more important as world tensions, anxiety and strain increase daily and millions seek vainly to "get away from it all." Inasmuch as all methods of hypnosis discussed in this book utilized relaxation as the first step, it should not be necessary to go over this material. Simply review the many induction techniques.

Lung cancer has become a very real threat to many people today, and the professional hypnotist is besieged with men and women who wish to curtail or quit smoking. This is easier said than done because smoking, although there are no physical withdrawal symptoms when one stops, is a strong, conditioned reflex and cannot (except in rare instances) be accomplished by the will alone. The best way to stop smoking is to make it an impossibility, and that is exactly what you do when you follow the method touched on in an earlier chapter.

All of us have tasted or smelled certain foods or medicines that nauseate us. The subject who wishes to quit smoking is asked to conjure up the vision and the actual taste and smell of the substances which upset his stomach and offend his nostrils, transferring its properties to cigarettes. This, of course, must be done under hypnosis. The subject then conditions himself in the following manner: One...This cigarette tastes and smells just like (mention name of repugnant substance). Two...It is the most vile and repugnant taste I have ever encountered, and I shall not be able to continue after the third puff. At the third puff, I will develop a paroxysm of coughing. Three...I cannot smoke the cigarette any longer, and I will have to put it out.

This sounds like a simple procedure, and yet it has worked for thousands. Some switch to chewing gum or candy, but the cure essentially lies in substituting one conditioned reflex for another. This is comparatively easy with hypnosis because, unlike narcotics, barbiturates or alcohol, smoking is purely a psychological addiction. There is no need for tapering off.

Stopping drinking, unlike smoking, doesn't involve merely the creation of a physical aversion to the drug. The patient's entire personality should be changed and more mature viewpoints substituted for the unrealistic and infantile viewpoints which lead to the addiction in the first place. The subject should give himself suggestions that he will be able to "face up" to the problems of every day life without recourse to the crutch of alcohol. It is a well-known fact that nothing is as bad as we think it is going to be once we confront it.

One of the strange aspects of drinking is that it is actually a form of self-hypnosis, and the cure lies in substituting a new viewpoint for the old. This fact can be demonstrated by the fact that drinking is begun in the first place so that the individual can be "one of the boys" or because it is the thing to do. Those who do not drink, at least as a social lubricant, according to this code, are "squares." Because of this, self-hypnosis must be directed toward reorienting one's sense of values. Sober reflection should convince anyone that the truly intelligent person does not drink to excess.

Nail biting is an unsightly habit, one that may even hinder one's social acceptance. The help lies in a therapeutic approach similar to that for cigarettes.

It is not hard to predict that many of those reading these pages are suffering from overweight. With 30 million Americans in this category, it has become one of the nation's chief health problems, and it is the predisposing factor in many other diseases such as heart trouble, diabetes, hypertension and atherosclerosis. If you are overweight, it is well to remember that (unless you are one in a million) you cannot blame your glands. The plain truth is that you eat too much.

We know today that overeating for some is an emotional problem, stemming from feelings of rejection and insecurity. Individuals who feel unloved, whether this is truly the case or not, make up for this lack to themselves by stuffing in large quantities of food. It would even appear that these people are masochistic, making themselves even more unloved by their gross gastronomical habits. A big factor in overweight in women is "raiding the refrigerator" while doing their housework. Most of them do this so unconsciously that they swear they eat less than most people.

There are a number of appetite-curbing drugs on the market today, but they should not be necessary for anyone who has acquired self-hypnosis. If you have learned to visualize yourself (visual-imagery) in different situations, you will have no trouble in picturing yourself having a slim, attractive figure, exactly as you were when you felt you looked your best. Keep this figure ever in mind and use it along with conditioning yourself against certain fatty and starchy foods. A trick used by some hypnotherapists is to have the subject purchase a dress or suit several sizes too small and then work toward being able to wear it. This actually has worked in many cases because it adds the element of competitiveness to the procedure.

Not all people overeat because of emotional problems. Some come from families where "licking the platter clean" was the rule because food was scarce. Others come from rich families where overeating by the parents established a habit pattern in the children. Certain races and nationalities look on fat as a badge of wealth and prestige, and children in such an environment are likely to be deliberately overfed. Regardless of the reason for overweight, however, the use of self-hypnosis is one of the answers to the problem.

Simple headaches, arthritis, neuritis and other painful symptoms yield readily to hypnotic suggestion. If physicians have given up on the problem and placed a subject on a maintenance drug dosage for pain, hypnosis can potentiate the drugs or even obviate them.

Two of the major uses of hypnosis are in childbirth and for intractable pain of cancer or some other incurable diseases. Although patients usually start with heterohypnosis, they are put on self-hypnosis as soon as possible, and there are many cases of women waiting too long and having their babies at home painlessly through self-hypnosis. The father invariably is the only one excited in such cases. The mother knows that she is an excellent subject and has been instructed in prenatal classes about every contingency that could arise. Inasmuch as stopping the birth pangs is similar to stopping other pain, the method should be learned so that it can be accomplished in a minimum of time.

The best way to stop pain is to let your right arm slowly rise while you are under hypnotic suggestion. Do not help it. If the suggestions are strong enough, it will "float" up. As soon as the arm is straight overhead, you should give yourself the suggestion that it is as rigid and unbending as a bar of steel. Following this, a suggestion is given that the hand is beginning to tingle and become numb. As soon as the numbness has spread through the entire hand, it will be insensible to pain. The hand is then placed against the part of the body where pain exists, and you will feel the numbness flowing from the hand to the affected area. This happens as a result of your suggestions and is the method followed by most subjects. Only a deep somnambulistic subject is able to remove pain by direct suggestion to the painful part.

There are many people today using self-hypnosis in the realm of sports, and an entire book has been written on improving one's golf game with this method. It is called *How You Can Play Better Golf Using Self-Hypnosis* by Jack Heise (Wilshire Book Company—Publishers).

Dr. Huber Grimm, team physician of the Seattle University basketball team, recently related the results when Dave Mills, a six-foot five-inch junior forward, asked for his help because he "froze" during competition. He had been benched on the eve of the West Coast Athletic Conference tournament in San Francisco. Spectators made Mills so fearful that he was afraid he would make mistakes—and in this frame of mind, of course, he did. Under hypnosis, Dr. Grimm suggested to Dave that he would be unaware of the spectators, be completely relaxed and would play exceedingly well. Dr. Grimm asked coach Vince Cazzeta to allow Dave to play and the result was astounding. Mills scored 60 points and cleared 63 rebounds, and his brilliant play led to his selection on the all-tournament team.

"All I did was free his spirit," Dr. Grimm reported. "He was in need of confidence, and I gave it to him through hypnosis." The Associated Press told the story as follows: "Dave Mills, a vacuum cleaner off the backboards, led a fast-breaking Seattle University team to victory last night. It was hard to recognize Mills as the same player who has been with the Chieftains all year."

Dr. William S. Kroger, a pioneer in hypnosis, undertook to improve the batting of a professional baseball player with equally sensational results. The player had been "beaned," and his fear of a recurrence was so strong that he became "plate shy." He had changed his batting stance so that he always had "one foot in the bucket" so that he could back away from the plate more quickly. He was given a posthypnotic suggestion that such an event happening again was exceedingly remote, and this was amplified by suggestions of confidence that he would immediately start slugging as well as ever. His batting average soared immediately.

Dr. Michio Ikai, professor of physiology at Tokyo University, and Dr. Arthur H. Steinhaus of the George Williams Laboratory of Physiologic Research in Physical Education, Chicago, have proved that track men can far surpass their best previous times under hypnosis. Their tests, incidentally, proved that there is no danger of an athlete going beyond his physiologic limit while bettering his former marks. They attribute the superior performances to the removal of inhibitions, which psychologically prevent an athlete from doing his best. This report was made before the International Congress on Health and Fitness in the Modern World held in Rome during the last Olympic games.

All reports, as a matter of fact, show that athletic performances are improved by psychological, not physical, means, and that built-in automatic reflexes protect the athlete against the danger of overexertion at all levels of awareness—hypnotic or nonhypnotic.

Psychologists are using hypnosis more and more to facilitate concentration and learning, and it is likely this use of the ancient science will become even more popular than its medical applications. The reason one learns so quickly under hypnosis is because of time distortion which allows you to obtain the equivalent of many hours of study in a relatively short length of time.

Undoubtedly, you have had experience with time distortion in your daily life. Remember how slowly time goes when you are not interested in what you are doing and how fast it speeds by when you are? And the drowning man, who sees his whole life go by, is an excellent example of this. Enough people have been saved to know that this actually happens. The point is that the subconscious mind does not record the passage of time the same way as the conscious mind.

The conscious mind records time physically, by means of a clock. It is objective and tells you that a thought or movement requires a certain number of seconds, minutes, hours or days.

Your subconscious mind has an entirely different concept of time that has nothing to do with the physical world. It is called subjective because your own sense of the passage of time is used.

Personal time varies according to the circumstances in which you find yourself. Haven't you noticed that when you are happy or extremely interested in something, time passes quickly? On the other hand, if you are sad or anxious, time seems to drag.

This is called time distortion. When you continue in a happy state, time is automatically shortened. When you are in a state of unhappiness, pain or anxiety, time automatically lengthens. This explains why the drowning man can review his entire life within seconds. Psychologists know this is possible, because your subconscious mind contains a complete record of everything that has happened to you since birth. Therefore, in moments of extreme distress your subconscious has the ability to distort and manipulate time.

If you have ever encountered danger or had a narrow escape, you probably experienced time distortion. Everything about you went into slow motion, and time seemed to stand still until the action was over. At that point, objective time started up again and everything returned to normal.

Many of you no doubt read an Associated Press report from Chicago on February 11, 1958, which reported how movie actress Linda Darnell had used hypnosis to help her with her first stage role. She had been asked to do the part on short notice and had no time for preparation. Miss Darnell telephoned her California physician for aid. He flew to Chicago.

Overnight, through hypnosis, Miss Darnell learned her part and astounded the cast by knowing everyone's lines. Not only did she learn the part, but she was coached in the character of the artist she was portraying. As a result, "Late Love" was a hit play. Miss Darnell was under the impression she had been learning the part for a week although only about 48 hours were involved and these hours were not continuous. After her first performance, she said: "I never felt so secure about playing a role in my life. Hypnosis helped me feel the part completely."

Imagine how much more we are going to be able to learn when study under hypnosis becomes widespread. And the best part of it is that the learning is in your mind for a long time. Forgetting or mental blocks that interfere with your recall of the information at any time, are reduced to a minimum.

In conclusion, I should like to recommend the entire field of self-hypnosis to everyone. It is a therapy which is positive, dynamic and constructive. An excellent example of this is contained in the autobiography, *Rachmaninoff's*

Recollections. In this book, immortal Rachmaninoff describes in detail his success in overcoming a severe case of mental depression. He had stopped composing and kept to himself, seldom leaving his room. After meeting with failure, using the available therapeutic remedies available at that time, he was persuaded by his relatives, the Satins, to seek the help of a hypnotist called Dr. Dahl. With much reluctance, he agreed to see Dr. Dahl and be treated specifically with hypnosis. Rachmaninoff's own words read as follows: "Although it may sound incredible, hypnosis really helped me. Already at the beginning of the summer I began again to compose. The material grew in bulk, and new musical ideas began to stir within me—far more than I needed for my concerto. I felt that Dr. Dahl's treatment had strengthened my nervous system to a miraculous degree. Out of gratitude, I dedicated my second concerto to him. As the piece had a great success in Moscow, everyone began to wonder what possible connection it could have with Dr. Dahl. The truth, however, was known to Dr. Dahl, the Satins, and myself."

Does this story sound incredible? You have the word of one of the world's greatest musical composers that hypnosis alleviated his severe despondency. This is proof that the emotions of the individual can be changed by the ideas he builds up about himself.

Dr. Leland E. Hinsie, professor of psychiatry, Columbia University, writing in his book, *The Person in the Body,* (W. W. Norton & Co.) states, "In some persons the fear of disease is often the only damaging evidence of disease, yet it can be so strong as to disable the person in all his daily activities." The entire field of psychosomatic medicine, which deals with the interrelationship between body and mind, has as one of its basic tenets that suggestion not only can cause psychological personality disorders, but many physical disorders as well.

It is, therefore, logical to conclude that the systematic use of positive mental attitudes in an organized, progressive, self-improvement program can be a vital influence in helping you lead a healthier life, both emotionally and physically.

Many people in need of help are at a loss as to where they can locate reputable hypnotherapists in their area. You may consult your family physician, county medical society or mental hygiene society. The chairman of the psychology department at your nearest college or university would usually have this information.

THE POWERS HYPNODISC

An effective yet inexpensive method of inducing hypnosis is with the aid of the hypnodisc spiral. In my book, "Hypnotism Revealed," a picture of the hypnodisc unit with the hypnodisc spiral attached is shown. Above is a picture of my latest hypnodisc spiral. I am now offering the hypnodisc spiral as a separate unit which can be used with your phonograph turntable.

The spinning spiral will cause a series of optical illusions, causing immediate eye strain and fatigue. The subject feels that he is being drawn into a deep, dark revolving cone. By your suggestions of hypnotic sleep, you can place your subject in the somnambulistic state very easily. With some subjects, hypnosis will take place almost instantaneously. This technique is often employed in stage hypnotism.

The use of the hypnodisc spiral is also an excellent method of achieving self-hypnosis. As you concentrate on the revolving hypnodisc spiral, you give yourself suggestions of hypnotic sleep. You will note the optical illusions as they occur and the pleasant, relaxing feeling that accompanies these illusions. Giving yourself further suggestions of hypnotic sleep, you find that you are easily able to attain the desired state of self-hypnosis. This method is one of the most successful and popular techniques yet known for achieving heterohypnosis and self-hypnosis. At the Wilshire School of Hypnotism, all students in the self-hypnosis class are conditioned with the aid of the hypnodisc spiral.

During my lectures, I place the entire hypnodisc unit on the platform without having the spiral revolve. Continuing with the lecture, I note individuals in the audience gazing intently at the hypnodisc spiral. Invariably before the end of the lecture, many will have put themselves into a deep hypnotic state. This group self-hypnosis was achieved without my mentioning anything about the hypnodisc. These individuals assumed that the unit is used to induce hypnosis and their looking at it with that thought in mind produced the hypnotic state.

The hypnodisc spiral is printed on firm cardboard, measures twelve inches in diameter, and has a hole in the center so you can place it on your own phonograph turntable. It has the general appearance of a twelve-inch phonograph record. I am sure that you will be pleased with your purchase of the hypnodisc.

Send for POWERS HYPNODISC
Price . . . $7.00

CASSETTE TAPES

ONE HOUR HYPNOTIC RECORDS ON CASSETTE TAPE	$10.00
ONE HOUR HYPNOTIC RAIN RECORD ON CASSETTE TAPE	5.00
TWO HOURS OF MENTAL POWER RECORDS ON CASSETTE TAPE	10.00

ONE HOUR HYPNOTIC RAIN TAPE (3¾ IPS)

One of the chief assets of a good hypnotist is to be flexible in his approach i hypnotizing his subjects. As you know, it is necessary many times to adapt a techniqu that is suitable to the subject, and not to make the subject adapt himself to th method of induction.

We know that with somnambulistic subjects any procedure will put the subjec under hypnosis immediately. The hypnotist gains complete control of his subjec just as fast as he wants. Unfortunately, most subjects do not respond at the fir session because of conscious or subconscious fears that must be gradually eliminate Once you get the subject to relax, or "let go," he will naturally succumb to hypnosi This is the problem that confronts all hypnotists.

Merely suggesting to the subject to relax or to "let go" is not sufficient, a rule, to bring about this desired state. The subject, at this point, cannot tui on or off his mental and physical state of being this easily. Even if we have th subject lie down, this does not assure the hypnotic state, as the subject can st be tense. Our problem is how to get the subject to relax. Our situation is sim lar to the physician telling his patient to go home and forget about a certa problem. I'm sure that you'll agree that the advice is virtually impossible to folloy

One of the major stumbling blocks in hypnotizing a subject, or in self-hypnosi lies in the fact that although we use words such as: "relax," "let yourself go," ar other similar terminology, the subject cannot readily put the meaning of the words into effect. It is difficult for most people to "let go" when we live in a socie that beckons us to "look sharp," "be sharp," "be alert," "be on the ball" and "mak every minute count." Emphasis on productivity does not lend to a society of relaxe individuals.

In my long experience as a professional hypnotist, I have tried many nov innovations for inducing hypnosis. Some have met with a great deal of succe and others have failed. It is difficult to determine the causative factors for succe or failure. We can only theorize.

I have used, over the last ten years, a technique that I shall describe now. Exce tionally good results have been attained with it; however, it is not infallible. It suggested to you as another good technique. In order to help the subject relax, have been using a one hour tape recorder recording containing the continuous sour of various degrees of rain. One half hour has a rain effect of very soft, light rainfa as on grass, canvas or tent top. The other side contains a half hour of a rain effect su as one would hear in a heavy downfall with prominent patter of water on pavemer

The subject is instructed to close his eyes and listen to the sound of the rain whi picturing himself relaxing near a warm, glowing fireplace. The relaxing effect th produced enhances our chances for success in attaining a deep, hypnotic state.

The tape will play on all standard recorders and comes recorded at a speed 3¾ IPS. The tape alone is worth $2.50. You therefore only pay $2.50 for the actu recording. **ONE HOUR HYPNOTIC RAIN TAPE . . .**

A PERSONAL WORD FROM MELVIN POWERS, PUBLISHER, WILSHIRE BOOK COMPANY

My goal is to publish interesting, informative, and inspirational books. You can help me to accomplish this by sending me your answers to the following questions:

Did you enjoy reading this book? Why?

What ideas in the book impressed you most? Have you applied them to your daily life? How?

Is there a chapter that could serve as a theme for an entire book? Explain.

Would you like to read similar books? What additional information would you like them to contain?

If you have an idea for a book, I would welcome discussing it with you. If you have a manuscript in progress, write or call me concerning possible publication.

Melvin Powers
12015 Sherman Road
North Hollywood, California 91605

(818) 765-8579

MELVIN POWERS SELF-IMPROVEMENT LIBRARY

ASTROLOGY

____ASTROLOGY—HOW TO CHART YOUR HOROSCOPE Max Heindel 7.00
____ASTROLOGY AND SEXUAL ANALYSIS Morris C. Goodman 7.00
____ASTROLOGY AND YOU Carroll Righter 5.00
____ASTROLOGY MADE EASY Astarte 7.00
____ASTROLOGY, ROMANCE, YOU AND THE STARS Anthony Norvell 10.00
____MY WORLD OF ASTROLOGY Sydney Omarr 7.00
____THOUGHT DIAL Sydney Omarr 7.00
____WHAT THE STARS REVEAL ABOUT THE MEN IN YOUR LIFE Thelma White 3.00

BRIDGE

____BRIDGE BIDDING MADE EASY Edwin B. Kantar 10.00
____BRIDGE CONVENTIONS Edwin B. Kantar 10.00
____COMPETITIVE BIDDING IN MODERN BRIDGE Edgar Kaplan 7.00
____DEFENSIVE BRIDGE PLAY COMPLETE Edwin B Kantar 20.00
____GAMESMAN BRIDGE—PLAY BETTER WITH KANTAR Edwin B. Kantar 7.00
____HOW TO IMPROVE YOUR BRIDGE Alfred Sheinwold 7.00
____IMPROVING YOUR BIDDING SKILLS Edwin B. Kantar 7.00
____INTRODUCTION TO DECLARER'S PLAY Edwin B. Kantar 7.00
____INTRODUCTION TO DEFENDER'S PLAY Edwin B. Kantar 7.00
____KANTAR FOR THE DEFENSE Edwin B. Kantar 7.00
____KANTAR FOR THE DEFENSE VOLUME 2 Edwin B. Kantar 7.00
____TEST YOUR BRIDGE PLAY Edwin B. Kantar 7.00
____VOLUME 2—TEST YOUR BRIDGE PLAY Edwin B. Kantar 10.00
____WINNING DECLARER PLAY Dorothy Hayden Truscott 10.00

BUSINESS, STUDY & REFERENCE

____BRAINSTORMING Charles Clark 10.00
____CONVERSATION MADE EASY Elliot Russell 5.00
____EXAM SECRET Dennis B. Jackson 5.00
____FIX-IT BOOK Arthur Symons 2.00
____HOW TO DEVELOP A BETTER SPEAKING VOICE M. Hellier 5.00
____HOW TO SAVE 50% ON GAS & CAR EXPENSES Ken Stansbie 5.00
____HOW TO SELF-PUBLISH YOUR BOOK & MAKE IT A BEST SELLER Melvin Powers . . 20.00
____INCREASE YOUR LEARNING POWER Geoffrey A. Dudley 5.00
____PRACTICAL GUIDE TO BETTER CONCENTRATION Melvin Powers 5.00
____PUBLIC SPEAKING MADE EASY Thomas Montalbo 10.00
____7 DAYS TO FASTER READING William S. Schaill 7.00
____SONGWRITER'S RHYMING DICTIONARY Jane Shaw Whitfield 10.00
____SPELLING MADE EASY Lester D. Basch & Dr. Milton Finkelstein 3.00
____STUDENT'S GUIDE TO BETTER GRADES J.A. Rickard 3.00
____TEST YOURSELF—FIND YOUR HIDDEN TALENT Jack Shafer 3.00
____YOUR WILL & WHAT TO DO ABOUT IT Attorney Samuel G. King 7.00

CALLIGRAPHY

____ADVANCED CALLIGRAPHY Katherine Jeffares 7.00
____CALLIGRAPHY—THE ART OF BEAUTIFUL WRITING Katherine Jeffares 7.00
____CALLIGRAPHY FOR FUN & PROFIT Anne Leptich & Jacque Evans 7.00
____CALLIGRAPHY MADE EASY Tina Serafini 7.00

CHESS & CHECKERS

____BEGINNER'S GUIDE TO WINNING CHESS Fred Reinfeld 7.00
____CHESS IN TEN EASY LESSONS Larry Evans 10.00
____CHESS MADE EASY Milton L. Hanauer 5.00
____CHESS PROBLEMS FOR BEGINNERS Edited by Fred Reinfeld 5.00

_____CHESS TACTICS FOR BEGINNERS Edited by Fred Reinfeld 7.00
_____HOW TO WIN AT CHECKERS Fred Reinfeld 5.00
_____1001 BRILLIANT WAYS TO CHECKMATE Fred Reinfeld 10.00
_____1001 WINNING CHESS SACRIFICES & COMBINATIONS Fred Reinfeld 10.00

COOKERY & HERBS
_____CULPEPER'S HERBAL REMEDIES Dr. Nicholas Culpeper 5.00
_____FAST GOURMET COOKBOOK Poppy Cannon 2.50
_____HEALING POWER OF HERBS May Bethel 5.00
_____HEALING POWER OF NATURAL FOODS May Bethel 7.00
_____HERBS FOR HEALTH—HOW TO GROW & USE THEM Louise Evans Doole 7.00
_____HOME GARDEN COOKBOOK—DELICIOUS NATURAL FOOD RECIPES Ken Kraft 3.00
_____MEATLESS MEAL GUIDE Tomi Ryan & James H. Ryan, M.D. 4.00
_____VEGETABLE GARDENING FOR BEGINNERS Hugh Wilberg 2.00
_____VEGETABLES FOR TODAY'S GARDENS R. Milton Carleton 2.00
_____VEGETARIAN COOKERY Janet Walker 10.00
_____VEGETARIAN COOKING MADE EASY & DELECTABLE Veronica Vezza 3.00

GAMBLING & POKER
_____HOW TO WIN AT POKER Terence Reese & Anthony T. Watkins 7.00
_____SCARNE ON DICE John Scarne 15.00
_____WINNING AT CRAPS Dr. Lloyd T. Commins 5.00
_____WINNING AT GIN Chester Wander & Cy Rice 3.00
_____WINNING AT POKER—AN EXPERT'S GUIDE John Archer 10.00
_____WINNING AT 21—AN EXPERT'S GUIDE John Archer 7.00

HEALTH
_____BEE POLLEN Lynda Lyngheim & Jack Scagnetti 5.00
_____COPING WITH ALZHEIMER'S Rose Oliver, Ph.D. & Francis Bock, Ph.D. 10.00
_____DR. LINDNER'S POINT SYSTEM FOOD PROGRAM Peter G Lindner, M.D. 2.00
_____HELP YOURSELF TO BETTER SIGHT Margaret Darst Corbett 7.00
_____HOW YOU CAN STOP SMOKING PERMANENTLY Ernest Caldwell 5.00
_____MIND OVER PLATTER Peter G Lindner, M.D. 5.00
_____NATURE'S WAY TO NUTRITION & VIBRANT HEALTH Robert J. Scrutton 3.00
_____NEW CARBOHYDRATE DIET COUNTER Patti Lopez-Pereira 2.00
_____REFLEXOLOGY Dr. Maybelle Segal 5.00
_____REFLEXOLOGY FOR GOOD HEALTH Anna Kaye & Don C. Matchan 7.00
_____30 DAYS TO BEAUTIFUL LEGS Dr. Marc Selner 3.00
_____WONDER WITHIN Thomas S. Coyle, M.D. 10.00
_____YOU CAN LEARN TO RELAX Dr. Samuel Gutwirth 5.00

HOBBIES
_____BEACHCOMBING FOR BEGINNERS Norman Hickin 2.00
_____BLACKSTONE'S MODERN CARD TRICKS Harry Blackstone 7.00
_____BLACKSTONE'S SECRETS OF MAGIC Harry Blackstone 7.00
_____COIN COLLECTING FOR BEGINNERS Burton Hobson & Fred Reinfeld 7.00
_____ENTERTAINING WITH ESP Tony 'Doc' Shiels 2.00
_____400 FASCINATING MAGIC TRICKS YOU CAN DO Howard Thurston 7.00
_____HOW I TURN JUNK INTO FUN AND PROFIT Sari 3.00
_____HOW TO WRITE A HIT SONG AND SELL IT Tommy Boyce 10.00
_____MAGIC FOR ALL AGES Walter Gibson 7.00
_____STAMP COLLECTING FOR BEGINNERS Burton Hobson 3.00

HORSE PLAYER'S WINNING GUIDES
_____BETTING HORSES TO WIN Les Conklin 7.00
_____ELIMINATE THE LOSERS Bob McKnight 5.00
_____HOW TO PICK WINNING HORSES Bob McKnight 5.00
_____HOW TO WIN AT THE RACES Sam (The Genius) Lewin 5.00
_____HOW YOU CAN BEAT THE RACES Jack Kavanagh 5.00

_____MAKING MONEY AT THE RACES David Barr 7.00
_____PAYDAY AT THE RACES Les Conklin 7.00
_____SMART HANDICAPPING MADE EASY William Bauman 5.00
_____SUCCESS AT THE HARNESS RACES Barry Meadow 7.00

HUMOR
_____HOW TO FLATTEN YOUR TUSH Coach Marge Reardon 2.00
_____JOKE TELLER'S HANDBOOK Bob Orben 7.00
_____JOKES FOR ALL OCCASIONS Al Schock 5.00
_____2,000 NEW LAUGHS FOR SPEAKERS Bob Orben 7.00
_____2,400 JOKES TO BRIGHTEN YOUR SPEECHES Robert Orben 7.00
_____2,500 JOKES TO START'EM LAUGHING Bob Orben 10.00

HYPNOTISM
_____CHILDBIRTH WITH HYPNOSIS William S. Kroger, M.D. 5.00
_____HOW TO SOLVE YOUR SEX PROBLEMS WITH SELF-HYPNOSIS Frank Caprio, M.D. ... 5.00
_____HOW YOU CAN BOWL BETTER USING SELF-HYPNOSIS Jack Heise 7.00
_____HOW YOU CAN PLAY BETTER GOLF USING SELF-HYPNOSIS Jack Heise 3.00
_____HYPNOSIS AND SELF-HYPNOSIS Bernard Hollander, M.D. 7.00
_____HYPNOTISM (Originally published 1893) Carl Sextus 5.00
_____HYPNOTISM MADE EASY Dr. Ralph Winn 7.00
_____HYPNOTISM MADE PRACTICAL Louis Orton 5.00
_____HYPNOTISM REVEALED Melvin Powers 3.00
_____HYPNOTISM TODAY Leslie LeCron & Jean Bordeaux, Ph.D. 5.00
_____MODERN HYPNOSIS Lesley Kuhn & Salvatore Russo, Ph.D. 5.00
_____NEW CONCEPTS OF HYPNOSIS Bernard C. Gindes, M.D. 10.00
_____NEW SELF-HYPNOSIS Paul Adams 10.00
_____POST-HYPNOTIC INSTRUCTIONS—SUGGESTIONS FOR THERAPY Arnold Furst ... 10.00
_____PRACTICAL GUIDE TO SELF-HYPNOSIS Melvin Powers 5.00
_____PRACTICAL HYPNOTISM Philip Magonet, M.D. 3.00
_____SECRETS OF HYPNOTISM S.J. Van Pelt, M.D. 5.00
_____SELF-HYPNOSIS—A CONDITIONED-RESPONSE TECHNIQUE Laurence Sparks 7.00
_____SELF-HYPNOSIS—ITS THEORY, TECHNIQUE & APPLICATION Melvin Powers 3.00
_____THERAPY THROUGH HYPNOSIS Edited by Raphael H. Rhodes 5.00

JUDAICA
_____SERVICE OF THE HEART Evelyn Garfiel, Ph.D. 10.00
_____STORY OF ISRAEL IN COINS Jean & Maurice Gould 2.00
_____STORY OF ISRAEL IN STAMPS Maxim & Gabriel Shamir 1.00
_____TONGUE OF THE PROPHETS Robert St. John 10.00

JUST FOR WOMEN
_____COSMOPOLITAN'S GUIDE TO MARVELOUS MEN Foreword by Helen Gurley Brown .. 3.00
_____COSMOPOLITAN'S HANG-UP HANDBOOK Foreword by Helen Gurley Brown 4.00
_____COSMOPOLITAN'S LOVE BOOK—A GUIDE TO ECSTASY IN BED 7.00
_____COSMOPOLITAN'S NEW ETIQUETTE GUIDE Foreword by Helen Gurley Brown 4.00
_____I AM A COMPLEAT WOMAN Doris Hagopian & Karen O'Connor Sweeney 3.00
_____JUST FOR WOMEN—A GUIDE TO THE FEMALE BODY Richard E. Sand M.D. 5.00
_____NEW APPROACHES TO SEX IN MARRIAGE John E. Eichenlaub, M.D. 3.00
_____SEXUALLY ADEQUATE FEMALE Frank S. Caprio, M.D. 3.00
_____SEXUALLY FULFILLED WOMAN Dr. Rachel Copelan 5.00

MARRIAGE, SEX & PARENTHOOD
_____ABILITY TO LOVE Dr. Allan Fromme 7.00
_____GUIDE TO SUCCESSFUL MARRIAGE Drs. Albert Ellis & Robert Harper 7.00
_____HOW TO RAISE AN EMOTIONALLY HEALTHY, HAPPY CHILD Albert Ellis, Ph.D. 10.00
_____PARENT SURVIVAL TRAINING Marvin Silverman, Ed.D. & David Lustig, Ph.D. 10.00
_____SEX WITHOUT GUILT Albert Ellis, Ph.D. 7.00
_____SEXUALLY ADEQUATE MALE Frank S. Caprio, M.D. 3.00

_____ MAGIC IN YOUR MIND U.S. Andersen 10.00
_____ MAGIC OF THINKING SUCCESS Dr. David J. Schwartz 8.00
_____ MAGIC POWER OF YOUR MIND Walter M. Germain 10.00
_____ MENTAL POWER THROUGH SLEEP SUGGESTION Melvin Powers 3.00
_____ NEVER UNDERESTIMATE THE SELLING POWER OF A WOMAN Dottie Walters 7.00
_____ NEW GUIDE TO RATIONAL LIVING Albert Ellis, Ph.D. & R. Harper, Ph.D. 10.00
_____ PSYCHO-CYBERNETICS Maxwell Maltz, M.D. 7.00
_____ PSYCHOLOGY OF HANDWRITING Nadya Olyanova 7.00
_____ SALES CYBERNETICS Brian Adams 10.00
_____ SCIENCE OF MIND IN DAILY LIVING Dr. Donald Curtis 7.00
_____ SECRET OF SECRETS U.S. Andersen 7.00
_____ SECRET POWER OF THE PYRAMIDS U.S. Andersen 7.00
_____ SELF-THERAPY FOR THE STUTTERER Malcolm Frazer 3.00
_____ SUCCESS CYBERNETICS U.S. Andersen 7.00
_____ 10 DAYS TO A GREAT NEW LIFE William E. Edwards 3.00
_____ THINK AND GROW RICH Napoleon Hill 10.00
_____ THINK LIKE A WINNER Walter Doyle Staples, Ph.D. 10.00
_____ THREE MAGIC WORDS U.S. Andersen 10.00
_____ TREASURY OF COMFORT Edited by Rabbi Sidney Greenberg 10.00
_____ TREASURY OF THE ART OF LIVING Sidney S. Greenberg 7.00
_____ WHAT YOUR HANDWRITING REVEALS Albert E. Hughes 4.00
_____ WONDER WITHIN Thomas F. Coyle, M.D. 10.00
_____ YOUR SUBCONSCIOUS POWER Charles M. Simmons 7.00
_____ YOUR THOUGHTS CAN CHANGE YOUR LIFE Dr. Donald Curtis 7.00

SPORTS
_____ BILLIARDS—POCKET • CAROM • THREE CUSHION Clive Cottingham, Jr. 7.00
_____ COMPLETE GUIDE TO FISHING Vlad Evanoff 2.00
_____ HOW TO IMPROVE YOUR RACQUETBALL Lubarsky, Kaufman & Scagnetti 5.00
_____ HOW TO WIN AT POCKET BILLIARDS Edward D. Knuchell 10.00
_____ JOY OF WALKING Jack Scagnetti 3.00
_____ LEARNING & TEACHING SOCCER SKILLS Eric Worthington 3.00
_____ RACQUETBALL FOR WOMEN Toni Hudson, Jack Scagnetti & Vince Rondone 3.00
_____ SECRET OF BOWLING STRIKES Dawson Taylor 5.00
_____ SOCCER—THE GAME & HOW TO PLAY IT Gary Rosenthal 7.00
_____ STARTING SOCCER Edward F Dolan, Jr. 5.00

TENNIS LOVER'S LIBRARY
_____ HOW TO BEAT BETTER TENNIS PLAYERS Loring Fiske 4.00
_____ PSYCH YOURSELF TO BETTER TENNIS Dr. Walter A. Luszki 2.00
_____ TENNIS FOR BEGINNERS Dr. H.A. Murray 2.00
_____ TENNIS MADE EASY Joel Brecheen 5.00
_____ WEEKEND TENNIS—HOW TO HAVE FUN & WIN AT THE SAME TIME Bill Talbert ... 3.00

WILSHIRE PET LIBRARY
_____ DOG TRAINING MADE EASY & FUN John W. Kellogg 5.00
_____ HOW TO BRING UP YOUR PET DOG Kurt Unkelbach 2.00
_____ HOW TO RAISE & TRAIN YOUR PUPPY Jeff Griffen 5.00

The books listed above can be obtained from your book dealer or directly from Melvin Powers.
When ordering, please remit $2.00 postage for the first book and $1.00 for each additional book.

Melvin Powers
12015 Sherman Road, No. Hollywood, California 91605

WILSHIRE HORSE LOVERS' LIBRARY

The books listed above can be obtained from your book dealer or directly from Melvin Powers.
When ordering, please remit $2.00 postage for the first book and $1.00 for each additional book.

Melvin Powers
12015 Sherman Road, No. Hollywood, California 91605

Notes

Notes